ONLY SOMETIMES
LOOKING SIDEWAYS

———◆———

THE BEST OF POLLY DEVLIN
selected from
IMAGE and *The World of Hibernia*

POLLY DEVLIN

Author, journalist, broadcaster, film writer, avid collector and planter of wildflower meadows, Polly Devlin has had a remarkable career, taking her far from her rural roots in County Tyrone into the sophisticated world of high fashion in London, New York and Paris.

As features editor for *Vogue*, she interviewed many major personalities of the sixties – Bob Dylan, John Lennon, Janis Joplin – and worked with renowned photographers David Bailey, Richard Avedon, Lord Snowdon.

She was married in Tuscany in 1960 to industrialist Adrian Garnett and they have three grown-up daughters. They share their home in Somerset with six dogs and have planted thousands of trees and reclaimed hundreds of acres for meadowland. Polly also maintains a house in London and in Dublin, which gives her an excuse to pursue another of her great interests – interior design.

In addition to her three acclaimed books, *All of Us There*, *The Far Side of the Lough* and *Dora*, Polly is also the author of the *Vogue* book of Fashion Photography and a book on ceramics for the National Museum of Ireland.

Only Sometimes Looking Sideways

POLLY DEVLIN

Foreword by Jane McDonnell of IMAGE

THE O'BRIEN PRESS
DUBLIN

First published 1998 by The O'Brien Press Ltd.,
20 Victoria Road, Rathgar, Dublin 6, Ireland.
Tel. +353 1 4923333; Fax, +353 1 4922777
email: books@obrien.ie
website: http://www.obrien.ie

ISBN: 0-86278-564-2

British Library Cataloguing-in-Publication Data
A cataloguing reference for this title is available
from the British Library

1 2 3 4 5 6 7 8 9 10
98 99 00 01 02 03 04 05 06 07

The O'Brien Press receives
assistance from

The Arts Council
An Chomhairle Ealaíon

Typesetting, layout, design: The O'Brien Press Ltd
Cover photograph: Colm Henry
Cover separations: Lithoset Ltd
Printing: The Guernsey Press Co Ltd

CONTENTS

ACKNOWLEDGEMENTS

I would like to thank Jane McDonnell for her help and encouragement; my grateful thanks also to Carolyn McGrath, Jane Matthews and Joan Grohman.

For Suzanne Lowry

FOREWORD

·······································

•

*L*ooking back over the last three years, it seems to me that the only occasions on which I remember there being utter silence in the editorial office at IMAGE was when, each issue, Polly Devlin's copy rolled off the fax machine. Assistant editor Carolyn McGrath and I knew better than to interrupt each other during that first reading of Polly's copy. Her pristine pieces provoked none of the impatient sights and muttered expletives often heard in the vicinity of our littered desks. The extraordinarily rich vocabulary and breadth of reference sometimes had us reaching for our dictionaries, but our absorption in her choice of subject, the elegant assembly of her thoughts and the intensely felt emotion and humour that permeate her work, was complete. For me, there is only one thing more revealing than reading Polly and that is talking to her.

Before we ever met, and before any of these pieces were written, I had been fascinated by Polly Devlin. When I joined *Vogue* as a novice journalist, I learned that this other Irish woman had preceded me, winning the *Vogue* talent contest at nineteen to embark on a career in the most glamorous magazine in the world. Years on, after she left, she was talked about a lot in tones of deepest respect by people of great authority, and I, although she wouldn't remember it now, was once assigned to ring her for some article or other with a ridiculous query about what lipstick she wore or whether she liked skiing. Her flinty observations and her kindness when she heard a kindred accent remained with me. After I joined IMAGE, I asked her to participate along with a number of other women writers, in a literary afternoon we hosted in Dublin; she held her audience, mainly women, enthralled. Their reaction to her was memorable and made a deep impression on me. I was encouraged to ask her to consider writing for this audience of Irish women through the pages of our magazine. When she agreed, I was excited – I knew her contribution would be very special, even unique.

Very soon, letters in response to her articles began to arrive from that 'constituency of women' who, as Polly says, are more or less like her, pre-occupied with family, children, married life, dogs, people, houses, gardens, poetry. She touches a nerve.

Her ability to write what women recognise as the truth about their lives owes much to her ability to cross divides. This collection of pieces from IMAGE (including one from our sister publication *The World of Hibernia*) reflects all aspects of Polly Devlin. Reading them again, I am stunned by their diversity, yet realise, as you will, that there is as much of Polly in the wife persuading her husband to sleep out in a field under the stars to satisfy a whim, as there is in Polly, friend of Jean Shrimpton, Peggy Guggenheim and Diana Vreeland; in Polly the Irish woman in her heartfelt reflections on the North, as in the mother delighting in the daftness of daughters.

Polly speaks to the wife, mother, daughter, sister, lover, thinker, dreamer in each of us. She illuminates in words 'the whole crumpled world in which working women and mothers live'. She authenticates our lives by writing them down.

In her introduction to this collection, Polly writes that, when she was writing for us, she was talking to someone who was listening, and listening *intently*. She is right; for there is no other way to listen to her.

JANE McDONNELL
EDITOR
IMAGE

SAYING SO TO SOME

One time, not that long ago, although suddenly it's a lifetime, Daisy my second daughter, and now a writer herself, asked, 'What is writing *for?*' She meant it as a genuine question, but all the same the question tore at me because the sub-text was, '*And* why is it more important than being with me?'

I remember reading Elizabeth Smart's poem: 'To be in a very unfeminine / Very unloving state / Is the desperate need / Of anyone trying to write', and agreeing; and wondering what the desperate need sprang from. Why do writers neglect life, children, love, and the reality of life in order to put a simulacrum of that life onto paper? Juvenal postulated in his *Satires* two thousand years ago that people wrote to cure the inveterate itch of a sick heart. Wallace Stevens, whose poetry I love for many qualities including its preciousness, wrote that the nobility of poetry 'is a violence from within that protects us from a violence without'. Both observations strike me as insights. But writing can do more; it can inspire, astound, estrange. And it can be valuable in a way that can't be costed. Our human and moral impulses are steadied and ratified when we read a good writer at work. So there's a goal and a half.

Writing has never been a major part of my life, though it has always been a major pre-occupation. *Ars longa, vita brevis* is as true a truism as I know, though my gloss on it is that life was always too interesting to leave and art too boring to begin. So a great deal of my time is spent in successfully avoiding writing. Most lives are full of more important things – family, children, married life, dogs, people, painting, conservation, trees, buildings, houses, gardens, poetry. So I'm delighted to find that, almost inadvertently, I have in these essays written about family, children, married life, museums, dogs, people, art, rooks and police brutality – among other things.

When I started to write these pieces for *IMAGE* I found that something else was happening; something very valuable to me, and, in analysing what it is, I remember back to when my daughters were babies and I was Chair of our local branch of the RSPCC (The Royal Society for the Prevention of Cruelty to Children). I remember that I was obsessed then with the vicious cruelty to children that still stalks our society, but that I paid little heed at the time to animal suffering – another theme in this book. I had been brought up in a country ethic where animals were creatures that fended for themselves and were lucky to be thrown scraps to eat unless they were being reared for money. Now I pay as much heed to one lot of living things as another and I don't think it is because my heart has grown harder. I'd like to think it has grown wider, levered open by having children. I think at some level the maternal instinct is a terrible and dismaying thing.

At that time there were, in the newspapers every day, more and more accounts of crippling cruelty to children. There still are; but my children were small then, so somehow I was the more stricken; it was to try and combat the hopelessness and helplessness I felt that I became involved with the RSPCC. As anyone involved in charitable fund-raising knows, the recurring dread is finding a Good Speaker for events. I was desperate to find someone wonderful to come and give a talk after our annual meeting in deepest Gloucestershire and cheer us up after the horrible statistics, and my dream choice was the jazz and blues singer, and writer and polymath George Melly. Anyone who has seen him perform, I think, could hardly fail to love him, he glows with energy when he's on stage, his pug face creasing with the sheer joy of living and hard drink and, although he's not surprised by any human villainy, he still loves humanity and its arts and crafts, no matter how artless, no matter how crafty. So, reader, even though I knew how busy he was, I asked him. But another of his characteristics is generosity, and typically he got to Stroud on time, delivered a diverting speech and left us all elated. Afterwards, I asked, rather hesitantly, if he would like to come to my house – some fifteen miles away – for lunch. I rather thought he would want to get straight back to London, a good two hours away – and I didn't want to put any pressure on him. (I do this all the time, couch an invitation or a suggestion so tentatively and with so many get-outs for the other person that they think it's half-hearted, when quite the opposite is true.) I could see George thinking about it – after all, if he accepted, his whole afternoon would go shoot.

We're going back a bit here – and name-dropping to boot – to when the Shah of Persia was still on his throne and his ambassadors were legendary hosts. I had been to a party in the Iranian Embassy in London a few days before (the very one that was besieged and burned in that famous and epic siege a little later), and afterwards (after the party, not the siege), the then Ambassador sent us two bottles of Krug and a tin – a very large tin – of beluga caviar. Now caviar comes in various guises, all of them expensive, but some more expensive than others, and the most delicious is not black at all, but like darkly shining grey pearls, just slightly on the move, and the price is frankly erotic. This is what I had in my fridge at home. The additions were a little lemon, some ice, some toast, and a cold bottle of the Krug. As we ate it, all blissed out, George said, almost crossly, just verging on delightful despair, '*But why didn't you say?* Why didn't you tell me about the caviar? *You never said.* I so easily could have said no.'

I remember his consternation now, when I look back and realise that I, too, after a delicious lunch in Dublin with Jane McDonnell, the editor of IMAGE, could so easily have said no when she asked me to write for her magazine. I had stopped writing for magazines and journals years before, when I began to feel that in writing columns I was behaving like one of those desperate insects that bite off their own legs in order to feed themselves. I would cannabalise myself for copy and then I would hate the opinionated look of my voice on paper, as though what I was saying was authoritative. In fact, the opposite is true – I never know what I'm going to say till I say it. I don't mean I just say whatever comes into my head – but what I say comes from a fusion of reaction and imagination and the working of the magma underneath; the source of one's opinions, knowledge, prejudice, wisdom or lack of it. Like George, I nearly said no and nearly lost my caviar – the rare, round, moving knowledge of what I was writing for. The *what* turned out to be a *who*.

I found I was writing for a constituency of people who were more or less like me. In much of my writing before, I felt as though I were talking into an indifferent silence – here, in these essays, I found I was writing lines to a listening post, into reverberations, echo and answer, answers often composed by women whose voices aren't generally heard. And when you aren't listened to, or your voice isn't heard, you get into the habit of not speaking, or else believing that what you are saying is not important.

Writing these essays has redressed this silence for me. One of the things I found missing in journalism and much of the media over the last twenty years is the voice of the women I heard in daily life around me, not strident, nor bossy, nor juvenile, nor selling brand names, but funny, querulous, witty, complaining, eager, resigned, wise and often old before their time; picking up their children from school, getting to work on the bus, or stuck in a traffic jam, shopping on the way to work or between school times, painting, writing, earning a living, sailing, climbing, exercising (or not), looking after children, eating to excess, scolding, loving, looking after old parents or dependants, and somehow fitting it all in whilst keeping their priorities right. They are living depictions of the humane moral impulses that motivate so many people's actions and yet are rarely seen as news-worthy or comment-worthy. In the 1980s and early 1990s they seemed under-represented in the outside world, the world of publicity, journalism, television. Women – as opposed to girls – seemed to become invisible, as though once they had reached a certain age they were edited out of the world's vision. Margaret Thatcher was on her throne but she seemed so oblivious to the very concept of sisterhood that not only was there not another woman in the Cabinet, but she had contrived herself into a female version of a man.

The literary world, the world of journalism and television was dominated by youngish men who reviewed each other's books, jokes and performances; it became a truism that they all knew each other at Oxbridge or wherever and over the years these chaps transmogrified into blokes, then into lads and doubtless will de-evolve into old, farting boychildren. The women columnists who were successful seemed their doubles, in a classic case of what I can only call *anything-you-can-do-I-can-do-bettership* (since there is no feminine equivalent for one-upmanship), and outfaced, outswore, outboasted and outbitched the men. The ones I met were whey-faced, etiolated and full of their own importance. The women – these women whose voices weren't being heard, whose work wasn't being shown – were their opposites. Funny, modest, deprecating. That, of course, was the problem. Modesty has no place in our society and society gets the representatives it deserves. That was one of the reasons why the election of Mary Robinson as President of Ireland was such a wonderfully heartening thing. Suddenly a humane, moral, older woman had power, was our representative.

In these essays I was given freedom to write what I liked and the result has no common thread or theme, but has to do with my own pre-occupations which turned out to be those of my readers. There's a wonderful line in Rousseau in which he talks of how you may have to force people to be free. Not being given any subjects, guidelines or requirements by my editor was a wonderful freedom, and I forced myself into it.

When you sit down and write freely you become someone other; the quest is to match up that other with the truthful interior you. I'm not talking about the confessional or the explorations of the psyche which constitute much of writing now, but rather what Robert Lowell called 'the grace of accuracy'. All my writing life I have tried to write truthfully, but the inherent showing-off within the act of writing always produced something different from the person behind the words. I always remember what Joan Didion, that consummate writer, called 'the act of saying "I, I, I," of imposing oneself upon other people, of saying "listen to me, see it my way, change your mind". It's an aggressive act, sometimes a hostile act.'

But I felt the opposite of hostile in writing these essays; I was reaching out to friends from a kind of isolation. Because, even though I was surrounded by my family, if you are a writer and don't write, you are deeply on your own. Writing these gave me back my voice. Not but that I didn't tune into a lot of other people's voices too. And in many of these essays I pay homage to earlier writers by incorporating their words into my text; such a practice, I'm glad to say, has an honourable ancestry – I don't want to hear any muttering about using or borrowing there, at the back.

Montaigne, that great essayist, wrote, 'I have gathered a posie of other men's flowers and nothing but the thread that binds them is my own'; (but what a thread). My thread is what was happening in a small world, but even so I left much out. Small mercies. In at least two of these pieces I write about my dogs – something writers are warned against – but I didn't write about how Archie, the little Dublin pug left to me by my old neighbour, has become one of the loves of my life, not only because of his hideous little face but also because his ineffable bravery (or stupidity) reminds me of the qualities I love in Englishmen. I scalded him with boiling water one day and, in panic, I held him under cold running water; he appeared not to notice his burn but was furious about the indignity of being doused in water. Another time he came running out to greet me, wagging his little, fat, round tail which was on fire, and never a furrow crossed his brow at the conflagration. (Well, I tell a lie, his whole face is one mass of creased furrow, but even at the height of the blaze it registered nothing more than his usual anxiety that one day I may forget he needs constant feeding.) And when our Aga blew up around him and we evacuated the house, he refused to budge from in front of it. Here too, I have written about a goldfish in New York but not about my life there, and about my favourite museum in Paris, the Nissim de Camondo Museum, but not about the one I love most of all, the Gustave Moreau house; all a matter of impulse, chance and space.

Another thing about this book: all writing is an assertion of uniqueness and mine is no different but, in these essays, for the first time, I felt I was writing home. Much of Ireland's literature is built on writing home, the emigrant's letters back, in whatever form it takes; novels, poetry, plays, letters and missives. And those who have not physically emigrated seem bent on the same quest – to go back to our lost domains.

For years I couldn't write home because I didn't know where home was. I had a family I loved in England (and I discovered that I was passionate about the houses that were my temporary homes – another theme here) but, partly due to my background and partly due to my emigration, and no doubt due to my own neurosis, I lost the ability either to feel at home wherever I was or to get back home to where I had been at home (wherever that was, some land of my dreams called Nostalgia).

I think that this sense of displacement and loss stemmed from the tense grip that the place called home in Northern Ireland, where I grew up in the fifties, had on me. That is perhaps something of a pre-occupation in these essays. As children, deep in County Tyrone, on the shores of Lough Neagh, we lived lives that had no quality of the transient, other than the future fact of death. That was a living part of our everyday life and an essential part of our religious Sunday; people were remembered on anniversaries, on the Month's Mind, after Mass and in our prayers. The ephemeral and the fleeting had as much reality for us in that lost world as the huge, lovely encumbrances that surrounded us – the barns and haystacks, horses, carts, trees and the people – still locked into a world where the horse was the fastest way of travel. Wordsworth would have recognised how we lived, Constable, even Breughel could have painted that beautiful, lost, raggedy, extravagant, untrimmed, hedge-laden world without any sense of shock, where roads were only little lanes winding between rose and bramble hedgerows, where houses lay far apart at the end of lanes or in their valleys, and the fields, many with fairy trees in the middle, were alive with insects and butterflies and filled with myriad grasses and flowers. Flax holes festered in the deep shadowed sides of the meadows and larks rose from stubble; the corncrake still craked and the flax crop spread a blue transparency across the land, as though the sky had dropped an outer veil. Vanished; all vanished. It lasted millennia and I witnessed it go.

I remember walking home from school and seeing the first poles carrying electricity to the district go up along the road; they were the narrowest, straightest, highest things I'd ever seen – apart from the dying poplars around Sarah Theresa's house down the road – and these new verticals were literally out of place. Even then, embedded deeply as I was in this intense Rousseau universe, I was always searching for somewhere else, where there was authenticity, resolution, credential and surefootedness, a solid base as it were, entirely different from the prospect before me and around me. I came from such an old and rooted place and yet I had no tenure on it. Something always seemed unmeshed, and I was always haunted by a sense of loss. Some of this is no doubt due to the tendencies of human nature, and some from an inherited strain in my father's family, and some, I am sure, because we are all exiles from happier lands.

But this sense of loss also came from something much less metaphysical, which was that we were, in a sense, exiles in our own country. We had an ancient Irish name and were living in our part of Ireland but we were British by nationality; all around us we apprehended an old Irish way of life and of doing things and of speaking, left over from the Gaelic, but at school we learnt only about the British way of doing things and seeing things. We breathed in our history, absorbed it, yet nothing native in us was validated or ratified by the authoritarian outside world. At home and around us we heard Irish music. Its complex harmonies and quavering grace notes had no value; the music we heard on the wireless was the only sound that counted. Except, of course, our hymns which were serenades to God and thus had a currency value. By reading, and through literature, I escaped from my universe into other universes. Reading was central to my life, but although I read what I could lay hands on, the work of writers who came from my native country in the true sense – writers such as William Carleton, John Slattery, Liam O'Flaherty, Gerald Griffin, Kate O'Brien and Maurice O'Sullivan, Lynn Doyle – was not there for children in the fifties in County Tyrone. Other odd things were though. I became an expert on how to dress a table for dinner for forty, using lilies and heliotrope and muslin festoons. I also knew how often housemaids should change their uniform each day depending on the size of the staff and knew too that, in earlier days, if a house had a pantry, it did not mean a small room with peeling pink paint as *chez nous,* but rather a house with a butler and housekeeper; I learnt how to mix a polishing paste using turps, beeswax and Castile soap, which receipt I still use today. All this arcane information and much more was culled from the ten volume set of unctuous Edwardian manuals on how a young matron should set up and conduct her household – part of my grandmother's library which had been banished to the loft.

There were a couple of seminal moments. One was when I found a booklet called *Townland Names of County Tyrone* by a Mr MacAleer, who had cycled through our countryside for his research. And there in a book – in a book! – were the very names of our townlands, so unofficial, so glottal; *Kilmascally,* the wood of shadows (and it *was* a dark and woody place), and *Killycanavan,* the wood of the wild or bog cotton, and lo, it *did* grow there and we gathered it to push up our noses. Don't ask. (The only worse thing was to eat the foam called 'cuckoo sally' which something laid on the back of sorrel and which was reputed to contains worms and which you could devour by accident.) To see those names set down for me was ratifying, not beyond words, but towards words; our place existed in the real universe of a book. Something stirred. The slow genesis that starts something off.

I remember my mother reading from Walter de la Mare's *The Song of the Mad Prince* ...

> Who said, "A Time's delight
> Hath she for narrow bed;
> Life's troubled bubble broken"?–
> That's what I said.

It was that 'I' coming in with such élan at the very last minute, the 'I' so powerful, so perfect, so unlike my own dear interior life, that struck me and had me hooked. In small secret notebooks I kept accounts, mostly aggrieved, of what was happening, and I thus became a scribe, as though I could, by marking it down, redress something or make it real. Later, in my teens, I wrote a kind of history of the Devlin sept, which was, I suppose, a kind of autobiography and thus a precursor of my first book *All of Us There*.

Some people think that the necessary prerequisite for an autobiography is an inflated ego: I find the opposite often to be true and the writer's ego has been so deflated that it needs to be filled up by his or her own evidence. They authenticate their lives by writing it down.

My first job was as a writer on *Vogue*. I was twenty-two. It was an odd transition from my world to that sophisticated one, but my previous existence, where things were called by their proper names, where manners were straightforward and oddly delicate, where I had not learnt any class consciousness, all made my transition into my new world much easier; it took me a while to learn of the great web laid lightly out over England – yet so weighing it down – that is upper-class familial and tribal connections. At that time the young women who worked on *Vogue* all seemed to know each other, not because they had been to school together (though partly that too), but because they had known each other from birth; their families were inter-related. It seemed to me an extraordinary coincidence that in this vast city of London, in a country of over fifty million people, so many people should somehow all know each other from the cradle and all be working in one building together. And when we went to lunch and were joined by girls from Christie's or Sotheby's or Colefax, they all knew each other too and talked of men friends who all had nicknames (as indeed they had too – Midge and Boofy and Pookie and Caro), names which, when I began to learn the new language, often concealed some great English name. I had no idea that I had wandered into an enclave, one of many, linked by the threads of the ancient woven net. I married a member of one such small enclave – he had gone to Eton and I was for a while deeply fascinated by their instantaneous recognition of each other, not because they had ever met nor because of the old school tie which apparently they only wore when travelling, but because of a myriad other signals, to do with stance, speech and the wearing of clothes and the cut of a collar. And if they carried a brown paper bag in the street they swelled up and died.

I was straddling two worlds. In that earlier life of reading anything I could get my hands on, *Vogue* had had a particular fascination for me. The big, fat, glossy magazine was a missive from another planet. I knew (in the way that fans know about the lives and habits of their idols without ever having met them) not only about Jean Shrimpton and David Bailey but the names of other more obscure models and photographers, writers, actors and musicians. I knew what people were purported to be talking about in the great cities of the world and what was on in the theatres of London, New York, as well as what various grand ladies were wearing to their dinner parties. The groundwork had been laid by those Edwardian volumes read in the soft, flea-ridden silence of the loft, and which had depicted an earlier, lost, ordered world. The key word was not glamour but order. The one outstanding feature of my world was its disorderliness, its chaotic quality. There were some immovable and serene routines – such as the herd of beautiful cows which each morning and evening swayed their slow way from their grazing grounds around the shore, a mile from the house, back to the byres. There the workmen, Paddy and Tommy, their heads pressed tight against their flanks, milked them, the stream of milk hitting the sides of the tin bucket in a steely cascade that turned to foam. But outside of these natural governing events, lay the chaos of everyday. I was fascinated reading Milton's *Paradise Lost* to find that Pandemonium was the capital of the kingdom of Chaos. Our large house set among its trees was Pandemonium, always filled with people and noise. Not much worked and if something broke it remained broken. I now know that the unavailability of skilled labour made repairs difficult; for example, at that time we were the only house in our district with an inside bathroom and lavatory, which meant that there wasn't much call in the neighbourhood for the trade of plumbing. But my upbringing gave me an enduring taste for orderliness and care.

When I opened the pages of *Vogue*, I was transported from Pandemonium into a celestial sphere. The world of *Vogue* was so brightly lit – everything was illuminated, the shine on a string of pearls, the gleam on the curve of a cheek, the sheen on a satin ball dress; at home the shine was the sun on the lough, the reflection of brass on the harness of a horse's neck, the gleam of leaves in the chestnut tree. In *Vogue* there were articles on cars as fashion accessories, E-type Jaguars; at home there were only two cars in the district, the priest's jalopy and ours. The world of *Vogue* sparkled night and day, flashlights, footlights, headlights. At home at night, the silence was palpable, the darkness profound.

One August I answered the questions set for the *Vogue* Talent Contest. The prize was fifty pounds – a fortune to me then – and a job at the magazine, but winning wasn't the point. I wrote because I was bored, it was something to do, and it was a kind of spear I shot into the air, like Longfellow, which might penetrate into that distant, impossible place. I never thought of it as a harpoon that would pull me off into the air after it and land me slap in the middle. To have a job at *Vogue* would never have entered my head as a possibility; as soon tell me to plummet into the future. A while later I went to London for the short-list interview lunch. I bought a black wool dress and put on a lot of mascara and pale lipstick. Lunch was in the monolithic Hyde Park Hotel and I knew everyone there by their names because I'd met them over and over again in the pages; that wonderful writer Mary Holland; the beauty editor; the editor herself. There they all were, almost real.

I flew back the same evening (Belfast Airport was called Nutt's Corner then and no-one of us found it even remotely funny). I think *Vogue* tried to telephone but, of course, we didn't have a phone, so they telegraphed. The next morning Joe Small, the son of the people who ran the post office, cycled over with the telegram saying I'd won. I wasn't surprised. The whole thing was so unreal, only not winning would have made it real; but then rejection has always had that ultimate credibility for me. And so it happened that one day I was on the bus to Belfast, and the next I was on the aeroplane to Tehran to interview the Empress Farah Diba. It was all as it should be; meeting Bob Dylan when he first came to England, or driving down the Champs Elysée in an E-Type with David Bailey on the way to see Catherine Deneuve. It happened. But it had never been my fantasy, I never thought it extraordinary. It was just the way my life had turned out. And regularly I went back to that Ireland where *Vogue* had no reality at all. There was no way to connect the two. Another parallel reality, echoing those earlier ones of my education.

I have led a dual life ever since, unable or unwilling to bridge the gap between the parallels. I like separateness. And, of course, I have made my philosophy fit the facts. I know now that wherever and how ever I lived, duality would be inevitable. I thought that my confusions and ambiguities about identity came from the political situation in Ireland and how it affected us and, of course, from our dinned-in religion. I thought my feelings were unique and artistic, but disconnection and dualities and loss are part of the human conditioning. You don't need to be Plato to know that the desire and pursuit of the whole is a quest for love.

When I was fifteen I went to the Gaeltacht to learn Irish and entered into a country that existed only in my imagination; the country, in a sense, that emigrants remember forever, even if they have never experienced it; a place where Irish was spoken freely and naturally and where people had the time of day for each other, no matter what time it was. I was as unhappy there, in Teileann, as I have ever been anywhere and learnt very little Irish to boot, but I do recall being well-pleased by learning of the variations in Irish on the verb 'to know': *fios* meaning 'common immediate knowledge', knowledge on the wing as it were; *eolas*, 'defined, rational knowledge'; *aithne*, used when speaking of knowing a person. The distinction seemed symbolic of Ireland and England to me, and I could have believed the Irish had a monopoly on the details of knowledge. But I knew too the meanings of 'apprehension', 'comprehension' and 'recognition' and myriad other English words, all naming the same conditions in depth of detail and all in English, both my mother tongue and my native language.

But with duality comes coincidence, though I don't call it

that and think of it as the visibility of connection. When I started work at *Vogue*, it seemed to me a world entirely separate from the one I'd left, but soon after I arrived there, I got a letter from Faber & Faber telling me of their excitement about a new Irish poet called Seamus Heaney. I was already excited since I'd known his work for some time – in fact, in 1962 in Belfast, I'd done a reading of his first poems with him, and in 1964 he married Marie, my elder sister, also a writer. I greatly admired his work, but, more importantly, what he was writing about was my landscape and original place too, yet what he could do with that *locus animae* was far beyond my reach. He seemed to have the place he grew up in within his grasp; he could not only accommodate it, but turn it into the stuff of dreams by showing its ordinariness. I saw too that he could rely on himself. I could make no use of this advancement in learning. All the gaps were too wide to jump merely by wishing, but it brought home to me that there was a way across the divide.

A couple of years after I arrived in London I began writing a column for the *New Statesman* and then for the *Evening Standard*; a dreadful and inexorable grind and one I regret if only because it's a dangerous game to play when you're young – to write about experience when you haven't built up experience.

From the first day I started work, I earned my living by putting words down on paper and everything I wrote was published. Nothing had any authenticity for me since I felt neither one thing nor the other, neither English nor Irish, without certainties, without answers, a cultural emigré, who had left family and friends, with nothing to posit my life on except my insecurities.

At this time I began to read the work of two other young writers, Edna O'Brien and Margaret Drabble, and the older Doris Lessing (although it was years before I read her great book *The Golden Notebook*, an articulation point for all women), these last two writers, at different times, resurrected that earlier intimation that there could be a path to find your way home. The answer *seemed* to be simple; a re-iteration of what I had seen in Heaney's poems: Find yourself and you're there. Not so simple, after all.

I remember the story of someone saying to Jonathan Swift, rather patronisingly, 'But, my dear Dean, after all is said and done, *Gulliver's Travels* is a very simple book to write.'

'Yes,' replied Dean Swift. 'Once you have thought of the big man and the little man, it is easy.'

Edna O'Brien was a fêted star in London and New York and she cast a shadow over any young woman from Ireland who was in the business of writing. She set up an image of Ireland that was powerful – imaginal poetics really. Her Ireland, her way of looking and feeling, had nothing to do with me, but it was inhibiting, especially what she once said about writing, to an interviewer, 'All the outings and adventures in the outside world won't do. You have to tap yourself, a form of blood-letting. It is very exacting.' Her Ireland, unlike mine, seemed full of passion and malice, strange men and adventure, alienation and shifts of the heart. Her place was foreign country to me, wickedly continental, and that was further revelation. How many blinding flashes does a person need? I was more inclined to take the Augustinian route. One day I would find my own place. But please God, not yet.

Then I read *The Summer Bird Cage* by Margaret Drabble. It's typical of what I was saying earlier that she, with her wholly womanly voice, should have fallen so heavily out of fashion when the blokes were running the show. She was castigated for her mundane tone, her diurnality, and certainly no-one could call her poetic; what you could call her though, was a brilliant writer and a confident one, who could found a world not so much on a grain of sand as in an unmade bed, or a visit to a hospital, or who wrote truthfully and believably of someone coming to a realisation of death because of opening a pedal bin. In *The Summer Bird Cage*, her first book, I heard a voice I was waiting to hear, a voice that said, 'This is who I am, nothing more or less, and this is what is happening to me.'

The key passage for me was when the heroine, who was wearing black stockings, was in a shop and a small child wandered over to her, reached out and started to pat her legs right up inside her skirt and thighs. What struck me was both that such a micro-event could constitute such a dramatic incident in a book (and it did, it did, I've remembered it for thirty years), and that that event was something small and everyday that might well have happened to the writer. She showed me that you didn't need the epic in order to be a writer; no-one, to my mind, had ever made such a tiny detail in a woman's life into the stuff of drama. I put out my hand, felt the string, the line reeling back to where life was happening to me. I found out I had a present tense in my life. The key thing too was that this authenticity had nothing to do with nationality, being Irish didn't matter, or rather was part of it all, no more or less. She seemed to me to define *being English*, but in reading her voice I recognised my own. She wrote with a certainty that what she had to say was interesting, and what she had to say was to do with women and their everyday lives and the growth of their souls, and she said it in her own quietly assertive voice. She was dealing with the whole crumpled world in which working women and mothers live, and which day by day they shake out and smooth out, and which for years leaves them with little time for anything else. Even if women have a room of their own, they have to keep the door open so that they can hear what is going on. Women need to listen. Much depends on that attention, but it makes for a split vision and a divided concentration and less time, and time is needed to write. Years in my case.

Yet the essays in this book were written in a short time and with no angst because I was talking to someone who was listening and, it seemed to me, listening intently. There is no greater gift for a writer. It took years for me to put pen to paper in the way these writers had shown, trusting to your own instincts, listening to your inner voice. Resisting the siren voices telling you that yes, indeed, writing is long and life is short. And I give thanks that so many writers wrote on and gave us the gifts of their writing, for writing at its best can make wonderful things happen. When I read lines like W.H. Auden's 'Altogether elsewhere vast/Herds of reindeer move across/Miles and miles of golden moss,/Silently and very fast', I know that words are a world, solid and miraculous, a world you can enter into. Auden has us up and running there, exhilarated in a way we could never do on our own. (Indeed, Auden can do this for me all the time, and it is from him that I have borrowed my title, perhaps in the hope that he will infect the book with something of his generous spirit.) And when, in that last inspired paragraph in *The Dead,* James Joyce takes us flying, magical and alarmed, across the plains and hills of Ireland, through the snow to the mutinous waves of the Shannon, then we know that language can transport the soul.

'All my life,' Colette wrote, 'I have gone to a great deal of trouble for strangers. This was because as they read my work they suddenly found they loved me and sometimes told me so.'

So there it is at last, the old avoidance. Love. When I began to write these articles, I, at last, was writing home to people I loved. I didn't have to explain myself, or apologise, or lead in with long preliminaries. I wrote to my friends who lived in the world I lived in, whatever the country, the place that Wordsworth knew. 'Not in Utopia – subterranean fields or some secreted island, Heaven knows where. But in the very world which is the world of all of us – the place where in the end we find our happiness or not at all.'

CAMPING IT UP

Out on the lawn I lie in bed
Vega conspicuous overhead
In the windless nights of June;
As congregated leaves complete
Their day's activity, my feet
Point to the rising moon

W.H. AUDEN

*P*icture this. It is a late summer evening in the gloaming, the curlew is calling and the hedges are dense, smelling, lit by the glow of woodbine. Our pasture field lies silent; the flying life that turns it into the Heathrow Airport of the insect world has gone to rest. From the woods that surround the fields come the last strains of the nightingales. All is still. Down the lane, between the hedges come two lunatics, trailing a motley selection of things, like rural Germans in search of a pool. They are carrying spindly, steel *chaise longues*, the uncomfortable ones, the ones that close up like a mousetrap when you lower yourself onto them or that snap and break your fingers. From about their persons drip blankets and sleeping bags and pillows. The man is making muffled, whining noises in his head which the woman can hear by divination;

sometimes the noises break through the sound barrier and become audible, a resigned, low grizzle; she is silent save for the odd snorting noise which anyone who has ever tried to suppress laughter (say, in church) would recognise as stifled, verging on hysterical. Following the pair are six dogs, completely agog about what is going on, barking and yelping fit to burst, grabbing each other and fighting a bit and, between times, rolling excitedly on badger droppings so a smell rises from them that is pale and livid. The sheep on the other side of the hedges stir and rise as the *caravanserai* passes onwards.

This odd pair turn into the big flower field, more than ten acres across and stumble across to the middle where they begin to pitch camp. Or rather, I, The Woman, Me – yes, 'tis I, and my husband, begin to try to put up the camping beds, which, of course, collapse and squeeze our fingers and crash onto the dogs who have become demented by excitement. By now it is nearly dark and we can't quite see what we're doing but finally, we get the bloody things up and climb into the sleeping bags artfully arranged along their lengths. As soon as we wriggle down into the bags, the beds jack-knife. The dogs watch with grave and silent interest as our heads hit our knees, high in the air.

We fling ourselves out from within the vicious grip, climb out of the bags, straighten the loungers, arrange the pillows and very delicately try again. This time it works but we are afraid to move so we lie side by side looking upwards to where a few crows, disturbed by us, circle on their way back to the wood, cawing their displeasure.

I remember a verse from Philip Larkin's poem – God, what a poet he was – about the couple, tum, tum de tum, how does it go – side by side, their faces blurred ...

> The earl and countess lie in stone
> Their proper habits vaguely shown
> As jointed armour, stiffened pleat

And that faint hint of the absurd –
The little dogs under their feet.

But they're not exactly the lines I want to remember. In any case, all poetic thoughts are flung out of my head as the dogs, who by now have almost swooned with pleasure as they finally realise they are going to be sleeping outside for the night, suddenly come to their senses, remember they have a job to do and start to bark; and bark; and bark. One stops, the other starts; a leaf rustles, they bark; an owl hoots, they howl; a fox cries in the wood, their voices become unhinged with excitement; a pheasant rises with a squawk, they fall into a frenzy. The noise goes on and on and on. I turn my head to try to see my husband, to try to read from his face what he is feeling, what the state of our marriage is going to be on the morrow. He hadn't wanted to do this in the first place. It was only because I badgered and fossicked about sleeping outside for so long that he is here at all.

This has been going on a long time. I've wanted to sleep out under the stars ever since John Brown and Maurice Whitten, boy scouts, cycled from Warrenpoint and came to camp on the lough shore. Such a thing had never before been heard of in Ardboe. It was 1954 and Warrenpoint was at least eighty miles away in County Down. We greeted them with the same awe and curiosity and caution as now we might greet a large, silver, saucer-shaped object full of little green men. Maurice and John, in fact, did look like little green men in their boy scout uniform and the glamour of the knife stuck down the sock knocked me out. My heart still misses a beat when I think of it.

Anyway there they were, aliens below the cross, camping out beside their small, green, pointy tent, looking at the stars and coming up to our house for milk. I yearned ardently, not after them, but after their sleeping bags, their palliasses, the whole enviable accoutrement stuff of the outdoors. We were brought up, as most children were in rural Ireland in those days, to regard the countryside as a place where men worked hard and left outside as soon as possible. I conceived a passionate desire to be a boy scout, again not number one social activity in Ardboe in the fifties when the October Devotions were the high spot of the season. I wanted to be a boy scout partly because of the knife in the sock but mostly because I wanted to sleep in the open. It seemed as magic a thing to me as, say, having wings. Somehow for such a simple ambition it never happened. Night after night I lay in my bedroom with the window wide open, listening to dogs bark at each other all along the lough shore round as far as the Battery, wishing I was out there with them in the dark.

Then when I left home the opportunities shrank. At the beginning, the men I was with tended naturally enough to be more interested in bed than in sleeping; and as time ran on, years later whenever I remembered the old craving, it was raining or freezing or I was in Hammersmith or Ballsbridge or Tenth Avenue and such environments aren't conducive; or whoever I was with had slept under the stars on the slopes of Kilimanjaro, in the sands of the desert or beneath the vast canopies of the Steppes and had no interest in a little rural excursion. Scoff.

Then in June, the most beautiful summer ever – day after day, night after night of balmy delicious weather – I finally saw there was nothing to stop me. It was reading that extraordinary poem 'Out on the Lawn I Lie in Bed' by W.H. Auden I quoted earlier that galvanised me and I knew at last not only that I could, but that I would, do it. I pretended, even to myself, I was going to do it alone, some secret tryst with my wild, untamed soul but I also knew fine well that at the last minute my husband would join me. Now there's a man who *has* slept out. We're talking here of a man who drove a train down the Orinoco Valley and slept on the footplate; there's not a continent whose open skies he doesn't know. So he wasn't exactly palpitating with excitement. In fact I knew the whole idea filled him with a kind of mild horror but he didn't complain and he knew that, at three o'clock in the morning in the middle of a big empty field, I mightn't be as brave as I was at six in the evening in a crowded house. So, being the man he is, he gathered his singing robes about him and came along. Sorry, read grizzling robes there.

The moon rose, the dew fell. I hadn't known about dew. I thought dew was a light misting, a little spangled dampness for the grass overnight, one of nature's kindnesses. Here is the interesting bit. The dew is like a very large, very dripping, very cold face flannel laid heavily along the surfaces of the night. It's like a large wet eel that slithers down your orifices no matter how tucked away they be. Dew pressed wetly into the corners of my eyes; dew soaked my hair; dew ran in runnels into my ears. And the more the dew fell, the more the dogs barked, partly to shake off the tidal wave of wet and partly because the night was alive with noise. From every corner came moanings and whinings and breathings and sighings.

Things nestled, pounced, fled, squealed, went silent. And every noise made the dogs more mad with excitement. Mona, the white bull terrier, barked the worst and, at one point, so desperate did my husband become that, braving the de Borgia-scissoring effect of his camp bed, he reached out, grabbed Mona and pushed her to the bottom of his sleeping bag where she hung deep, like a large suspended sausage over the bottom rail. At least she was silent, though I thought that might well be from suffocation. We didn't sleep. We lay like the stone couple staring at the studded, scudding sky, listening to the cacophony.

The clouds came over and hid the stars and a keen wind sprang up. At five o'clock the birds woke and began their thunderous chorus. 'Are you awake?' I asked.

'Awake?' he said incredulously. 'Am I awake?'

'Can we go home?' I whispered.

With one bound we were off our beds and had flung ourselves out of the manky sleeping bags. We were dripping wet and frozen. Mona crawled up from the depths of her pit, well pleased with herself and turned around and around in a white spinning circle while the rest of us shook ourselves, shivered and began the long trek home. From a neighbouring field, I saw an early morning farmer watch us, his mouth opening and closing, then turn and run on his little stumpy legs to try to get Mrs Farmer out to share the fun before it disappeared. I could have told him he had plenty of time. We could walk only very slowly, like old clockwork toys whose joints have rusted up.

We crept home through the glittering lane but, as we reached the house, the dogs thought it best to warn everyone. They all looked out of their warm windows and laughed at us, openly, for all I've done for them over the years. Fortunately, I come from a proud people and ignored them and went to bed.

All the same, it was worth it. I had slept out and I had caught the bug. Now this year, all spring and, I hope, the rest of the summer, I sleep out every night in a perfect compromise or *camp*romise, as my daughter calls it. I bought an Irish gypsy caravan (or van or wagon as I now know I must call it – never caravan) from Spence MacKeown in Tyrone, which a man from Castleblayney with a cigarette in his mouth and fearlessness in his blood, hitched onto a trolley and bowled along the motorways to bring here, pursued by police whom he shook off without a bother on him. It is painted and decorated and has a pair of lanterns and a place for a bale of hay and I sleep out in it most nights, watching out from under the hooped canvas, dry and snug but in the open air as the moon rises. The dogs sleep on the ledges and steps and being above ground seems to mean they can relax and stop barking occasionally. The sheep sleep underneath and shift and stir in the dark. The cuckoo calls sometimes, an amazing sound in the night, and the owl and the wood pigeon. Sometimes the air is torn by a dreadful fight between two creatures, and the dogs are instantly alert. So am I, it sounds like blue murder. But I go straight back to sleep. I have become so accustomed to these strange sounds of the night air that they accompany me into my dreams. Before I sleep I think of that old lough shore and the little green tent and Maurice and John camping and my longing to join them and watch the moon rising over the water and see it climb all night. And, as I drift to sleep, I remember those Larkin lines I couldn't remember on that first disastrous night *en plein air* when the man I love loved me enough to share the dew and my dreams or, to be truthful, the lack of them:

> ... and to prove
> Our almost-instinct almost true;
> What will survive of us is love.

ROOKS

They'll start building their nests tomorrow,' he said, looking out the window at the constellation of rooks, watching their undulations, sinking downwards and then sheer up, flapping, shifting, settling, swaying on the edges of the tall old trees around the house where I grew up, the family house, like crêpe decorations at Dracula's house.

'Why tomorrow?' I said.

'It's the first of March,' he said, 'their anniversary, and they always start then, except if it's a Sunday. They won't start on a Sunday.' He was the sanest of men except when he was dealing with folklore, superstition and charms. And now we're coming round to believing in what he believed in – what so many of his generation and generations before, reeling back into history, believed in, before we got so clever and so cynical – the magic that has nearly been lost, of the cures and charms that were intrinsic and corporeal in our lives when we were children, but are now so rare as to be almost vanished. A charm was a gift, an attribute for a particular form of healing, often passed down from one member of a family to another, and the custodian of such healing and charming gifts often possessed a seer's vision, knowing in advance what form of cure would be needed before a formal request was made. When I was a child in my country district, as many people went to have their own illness or that of an animal charmed away as went to a vet or a doctor; and all the many children with warts at school had them charmed off. But then again, who has warts now? No regrets there, which makes a change for me.

I went out to look at the preparations the rooks were making for their vast new nesting operation on the morrow, but they seemed as impudently relaxed as ever, apparently undriven by any biological urge other than to behave like the hooligans of the bird world, raucous, bullying, swaggering on the wing.

In fact, they looked and sounded as they always do, handsome scoundrels, small-time gangsters, hanging around the street corners of the sky, giving any passer-by a hard time and the once-over, making a real racket about it. The idea of them starting to build a cosy nest the next day seemed fairly improbably.

'You should always tell the rooks the news in the house,' Willie said. Willie knows all the folklore; if he gets stuck he makes it up.

'Surely you mean the bees?' I said. 'You tell the bees.'

'Not a hait of the crack,' he said. 'You wouldn't tell themens anything, they'd sting the face off you as soon as listen. It's rooks you tell; if you don't and then the thing happens, they'll leave and build their rookery someplace else.'

I tried to think of some vast, exciting piece of news I could withhold from them, to occasion the sulk and the exodus.

'Rooks have schools,' Willie said, 'there's times when they'll all be perched on the branches sitting and not a peep out of them and that's when they're teaching the young.'

If those are schools, I thought, then they were not unlike the

schools I sometimes see let out on London for a day-outing –
anarchic, heaving swarms of pupils with a defeated teacher, lost in
the muddle, trying to make himself heard.

'They say that if they leave a house it's bad luck,' my father
said.

'That's the honest truth,' Willie said. 'There's not a house
they left that's not derelict.'

I did not say that, as is so often the case, philosophy can be
made to fit the facts and vice versa and the sad, raw history of
Ireland is tied up with folklore and superstition. Only bigger
houses in this land-hungry country had the stand of trees, the
plantations necessary to support a rookery. And since many of the
big houses had suffered neglect and depredation, had been burned
or had fallen into ruins, and the rooks had been frightened off or
starved out, the dereliction had very little to do with them either
coming or going. But this was wisdom after the event so I kept my
peace.

'I would miss them if they left,' my father said.

I thought how much I wouldn't. That incessant cawing that
punctuated my childhood; the muddle of sticks on the lawns; the
endless circling shapes against the sky, the vast flurries when they
all poured themselves upwards at some internal alarum, the early
morning chorus, the way they ruined the trees, tearing at the
branches.

And I thought too, of how quiet the place would be without
them and how lonely, and how much my father loved and
celebrated them as he loved and celebrated so much, seeing
interest and amusement in things that I, left to myself, would only
find irritating. He could always shift the world a little on its axis by
the nudge of his humour.

I was going back to England and I was frightened. Before I
left, I went down under the trees and told them I had no news and

didn't want any news; all I wanted was that he would see them build their nests for a little while longer.

'You were down with them all the same,' he said, when I came back in. 'What were you telling them?'

'Nothing,' I replied, and he looked at me sharply.

'Do you remember what your mother used to recite ... "I climbed a hill as light fell ...",' he hesitated.

'"As light fell short,"' I prompted, the tears about to trip me.

'"Short",' he continued, pleased. '"Short ... And rooks came home in scramble sort; and filled the trees and flapped and fought, and sang themselves to sleep." Whoever wrote that had looked their fill at rooks all right.'

To cover the moment, I said, 'You couldn't exactly call it singing.'

'I do, daughter,' he said, 'it's singing to me. I'd hate not to hear them singing themselves to sleep.'

The next morning, as I drove away along the road by the lough shore, I saw one rook and then another and another, a kind of disconnected rosary of black shapes, fly to the top of the trees with twigs and straws in their beaks. It was the first of March, it wasn't a Sunday, and I knew he would be at the window smiling.

I went back again this year, on a different kind of anniversary, and there they were, busily about their nests as though nothing had happened. I went down to them perched in their trees, and I told them, and I told them too there was no-one left who thought their noise was singing and, as I watched their great black wings rising in scramble sort, I remembered those lines from 'In Memoriam': 'The last red leaf is whirl'd away, The rooks are blown about the skies ...' and their movement and colour matched my mourning.

THE BLACK NORTH

A phrase I rarely hear now is 'the Black North'. Yet, when we were children, spending holidays in Bray and Greystones, and were introduced to elders, they would say, 'Ah, from the Black North'. I discerned even then that these kindly people did not think we were really from Ireland. We were from the Six Counties, the Black North, Ulster. In all my years I never heard anyone ever ask any child if they were from Connaught or from Munster, yet we were always provincial. As a child, I didn't know enough to say, 'I'm from Tyrone, once the most Gaelic of all counties, and what's more, over a thousand of my sept died fighting for The O'Neill, fighting to keep the old Gaelic order alive, or to put it another way, fighting for our lives.' Well, of course, I didn't. I didn't know about it, for a start.

Last year when I visited Killarney, I went on local radio and was disconcerted to be interviewed as if I was from a foreign country. 'Would you ask me those questions,' I asked the interviewer (mildly enough, mark you), 'if I was from Wexford?' She agreed she would not. They were not topographical, you understand, but cultural questions, as if I came from a place where they ate camel kidneys for breakfast. And in a sense we do; there is a difference between the Irish in the South and the Irish in the North. There is a kind of black humour which long predates the Troubles ... all the perversity of living in a climate of antithetical values has become distilled into a particularly sour cast of humour which, having been reared on it, makes you despise the humour of other countries. Half the time, in Ulster, you do not know whether to laugh or to cry and, within the space of that choice, Ulster humour lives.

My dear friend Suzanne Lowry, also from Ulster and who lives in Paris, flew to Belfast to do a story, then took the train on to Dublin. The train hissed into Portadown and stopped. There was complete silence. She thought of 'Adlestrop'. Sit up straight there. Everyone knows 'Aldestrop', it is just about the most famous poem in the English language (except for bloody 'If'), one of the simplest, one of the most evocative:

> Yes, I remember Adlestrop –
> The name, because one afternoon
> Of heat the express-train drew up there
> Unwontedly. It was late June;
> The steam hissed. Someone cleared his throat
> No-one left and no one came ...

Suzanne recited the poem to herself; 'No-one left and no-one came' seemed particularly appropriate. Finally, because she had an appointment in Dublin and time was wearing on, she climbed onto the deserted platform and spied a uniformed official. She tracked him to his lair, priming herself as she drew near, because she lives in Paris where trying to complain to an official is like trying to carve stone with a teaspoon; no impression, no reaction, no point; just exhaustion. 'I want to complain,' she said.

His face lit up. He leaned back in his chair and smiled at her beatifically. 'Complain away,' he said.

She knew then she was really back in Ulster where there is an accommodation of life's foibles among the Irish. They have had to accommodate so much that was inhuman that the odd human quirk is welcome enough. Humour there is antennaed to ridicule pretension and stupidity and slow wittedness. I remember years ago there was to be a coupling in space of a small craft and a larger one, which went terribly wrong. It was rather like watching a sci-fi version of *The Graduate*, a small, shy, round thing spinning away whilst at the same time yearning to reach a bigger, older, desirable object. The control room at NASA was full of anxious faces and the commentators and spokesperson were puzzled and bemused by what could have happened. There were shots of the small space craft now lying forlornly, legs in the air upside down in space. 'We can't tell what has happened,' they mourned.

'I can tell them quick enough,' my father said. 'It's *couped*.'

There is a wonderful dour pessimism inculcated in people of all religions in the North and a kind of grim obeisance to misfortune. 'You'll come on them,' a driver of a car would say if another car overtook him on the road. (I'm talking of in my day – now, you understand, they would drive over you as quick as look at you.) What the driver meant, nay, wished for, was that the car that had had the bad manners to overtake would be found in a ditch, its occupants punished with a broken leg or two. Nothing serious, just enough to teach them a lesson.

I went to Belfast not long ago to appear on a TV show, a full day's travel for a five-minute appearance, and stayed in a hotel that had been bombed, and I shouldn't wonder if it wasn't bombed because of the food.

I went downstairs to have a meal and found myself in a

restaurant festooned with old placenames from defunct Ulster railway stations (which is what brought the Suzanne story to mind). I was finishing my meal, or rather leaving it, and thinking, though idly enough, about complaining (for it's not every day you meet a man like the one at Portadown station), when I saw the young and shy English businessman on my right having a problem with a ravishingly pretty waitress. They had eyes for each other but she wasn't lettin' on.

He was asking her if they had brown bread.

'We have surely,' she said. 'Lovely wheaten bread.'

'But have you any *brown* bread?'

She looked at him as though he was mad. 'Didini jus' say we have wheaten?'

He looked agonised, as well he might because what she was saying was '*weeden brayed*' with her voice rising in that curiously Ulster way that makes statements sound like questions. 'I'll have some of that,' he said, cowed. She went off and he saw me looking at him. He leaned over. 'What is "*whidden*"?'

I didn't dare try the same run of vowels. 'It's whole wheat bread,' I enunciated, and he looked relieved.

'And that's the Ulster name for it?'

'No,' I said. 'That's the Ulster pronunciation.'

When she came back with the wheaten bread and soda bread (the best bread in the world, I do believe, is baked in Ulster), he ordered the sukiyaki. A bad mistake, I could have told him, but nobody likes a smart alec. I knew what it was like because I had had it just before. I was given a hot plate, *very hot,* and a few minute later the stuff itself was brought on, erupting and sizzling on a griddle; it gave every appearance of being not only edible but delicious. I don't know what it was but it wasn't food. Anyway, I held my peace and he ordered it, he was duly brought the empty, hot plate by the beautiful girl, who, as she juggled it in front of him, also blew on it very hard to cool it down; as she put it in front of him, she gave him a warning.

'See you,' she said, 'that plate, you touch it and it 'ud sear you.' She leaned over and blew on it again.

He looked at me desperately for interpretation. A sprig of parsley on the hot plate was curling up with the heat like a human being putting his feet into too hot a bath. He stared at the empty plate and then at the girl, and she looked back as beautiful as a bad angel. I could see he wanted to ask where the actual food was and so could she.

She said, triumphant, 'That's all yer gettin'.'

Just then, the chef ran out with the scalding sukiyaki (which he hadn't done for me) and emptied it out. I looked long and hard at this chef to see if he, who thought this stuff was food, was wholly human. The young man ate up his sukiyaki. He was what my father would have called 'manful'. Later on, I saw him and the waitress communicating quite well without words.

I remembered a story of Hugh Shearman's, an Ulster historian with a distorted view of Ulster (in a long book, Tyrone was dismissed in about three pages), in which he compared the Dublin waitress's enquiry of 'Have you given your order?' with the Belfast one of 'Yi getting?'; and the Dublin waitress asking a customer in her way, 'Excuse me, please' and the Belfast one, 'Wud ye mind stanninn' out of the road?' There is a laconic quality to many dialogues in Ulster.

My sister Helen got onto a train in Dublin, hoping it was bound for Belfast. Again no-one to ask so she said to the elderly, decent man with his hands on his knees, already ensconced there, 'Is this the train for Belfast?'

He did not look at her; when he spoke he had an Ulster accent. He said, 'I take it to be.' She settled herself in and they both went to Belfast without another word being exchanged.

My favourite Ulster story is of a man going up to the door of a house where another man was standing and asking, 'Is Jimmy in?'

'No, he's not in.'

'Why's he not in?'

'He's dead.'

'Did he say anything before he died about a wee pot of red paint he had of mine?'

I've never met an Ulster-born person who doesn't find that funny. I tell a lie. I've met a few who thought it a perfectly reasonable request. Part of its humour lies in its melancholia and its meanness. The Black North. No Catholic in Ulster but would know that the story is about a Protestant in much the same way stories of tightfistedness in England are about Scots. Pure prejudice of course. *Of course.*

I never go back to Ulster but my heart lifts. I go back to my own small townland; people born in the country of Ulster are passionately connected to their townland; someone from Farsnagh is different from Aneteerbeg; although you could cover both places with a big handkerchief, you feel the difference as much in character as in geography. We were from Sessiagh, but its real name was *Muinterevlin,* 'the country of the Devlins'. I know now why people are so passionately attached to their townland in Tyrone and Derry, though I didn't know it when I was growing up. It was all they had left. 'Ulster Names', a poem by John Hewitt, is glorious to recite ...

> The names of a land show the heart of the race;
> they move on the tongue like the lilt of a song.
> You say the name and I see the place –
> Drumbo, Dungannon or Annalong.
> Barony, townland, we cannot go wrong.

Ulster was such an odd place to grow up in. Perhaps the Killarney interviewer was right and we are from a foreign country. Sarah, who looked after us as children, was obsessed by the Free State. She only listened to Athlone radio station, which gave us an idea of a mystical place, an *Ultima Thule* where they had Gateau cakes for tea and, if you felt like singing, you *did* sing an Irish song, and the trains were searched at Goraghwood. Were we even Irish? We were taught no pride in our history at school. We had no 'our history'; the only history we knew was English history; one of the few Irish songs we were taught was a mysterious thing which went 'My love's an arbutus by the borders of Lene'. Who knew what that was about? Not me.

Later on, when I was sixteen, I wrote a potted history of the Devlins culled from a book on the Devlin sept, published by a professor from Pennsylvania. I produced a neat little bit of plagiarism, but all the same it fired me into writing, and reading it now, I see a young woman trying to decipher her place in a world which apparently had very little place for the likes of her. What I learned from that book, and another one called *The Ulster Clans* by T.H. Mullin and J.E. Mullin, about what had happened to us, to the clans and septs of Ulster, made the blood boil with rage and pride. The royal clans of Ulster, the O'Neill and McLoughlins, descended from Murdock MacEarca, the O'Devlin and O'Donnellys descended from his grandson, the Quins and O'Mellans and the O'Hagans, all noble stock, all neighbours, all reduced from their national station, and their history never mentioned because for years it was too painful, so that finally it sank and lay buried.

In his *Plantation of Ulster*, Hill wrote;

> ... when the native gentry lost their homes and houses they received short shrift; anyone found lingering around their old homes could expect to be

> shot ... the British settlers generally do not appear to
> have had any kind thoughts or sympathies; for that
> class who had been more respectable than themselves
> they naturally cherished a vague terror ...

I know the feeling. Many's the time I've sat beside it in the Six Counties. 'We may imagine something of the agony and dismay of those who had occupied positions of comfort and respect throughout the several counties of Ulster but who were doomed to be out cast on their own soil ...'

I remember on his radio show, Gay Byrne asking me what must it have been like to have gone straight to *Vogue* from my place and background; *where* I lived he said, but I think he meant *how* I lived. I wanted to show him pictures of my ancestors – tall, dark, mannerly men and women, wonderfully turned out; my grandfather in his Panama, shoes polished till they gleamed, his walking stick and dog beside him. But the whole thrust about the Irish in Ulster was that they lived in a bog and ate stirabout. Sometimes I think it is called the Black North because the whole place is steeped in melancholia; bad karma, people would say. I mean if you read of the conquest of Ulster under Mountjoy, it turns your guts. The official policy was the utter devastation of the countryside until people starved to death and so resistance ended. Fynes Moryson, Mountjoy's secretary, wrote of multitudes of people dead with their mouths all coloured green by eating nettles and docks and tells us of how he put the scorched earth policy into practice:

> Where other deputies used to assail the rebels only in
> summer time, this lord persecuted them most of the
> winter ... this brake their hearts for the air being
> sharp and they naked and they being driven from
> their lodgings into woods bare of leaves, they had no
> shelter for themselves. Besides that, their cattle

giving them no milk in the winter were also wasted
by driving to and fro; and they being troubled in the
seed time could not sowe their ground. And, as in
harvest time, both the deputies forces and the
garrison cut down the corn before it was ripe, so now
in winter time they carried away or burned the stores
of victuals ...

It's easy to say forget, forget, but hard to do if it happened to your
ancestors.

There are other things lying buried in the North besides
hurt, grief and resentment. In a place called 'the Brack of Gelvin',
a couple of miles from Dungiven, where a great battle took place
as part of the 1641 rebellion, a man cutting turf in 1753 uncovered
a man's body stretched full length, dressed in full dress tartan
uniform and cloak. And I remember being fascinated by the story
of the O'Cahan or Kanes coming every year throughout the
eighteenth century to dine on the grass outside the ruined walls of
their castle at Ballylough. At their meal, they renewed their claim
to their ancient family possessions.

Pain upon pain upon pain. A poet once wrote of the discreet
greys and browns of the Ulster character but there was nothing
discreet or grey about the place we grew up in. Aahh, no daughter
dear, as the old people used to say, it was not called 'the Black
North' for nothing.

THE STAG OF THE STUBBLE

*L*et us now think about the hare. I don't know why it's always called the 'mad March hare' since you are far more likely to see one in April, the fool's month and none the worse for that. Not that you are likely to see one. Stand up all those who have seen a hare, really seen one. Do you know what an Irish hare looks like? It has a yellowy orange fur, a rusty look, rich as a fox, not glossy, but reflective of many shades of light; the tail, fluffy and entire; white both in summer and winter; the furry soles of the feet are brownish. So. Now let me tell you that your chances of seeing one are rapidly diminishing because hares are too. If you remember them from your childhood, then treasure the memory. Soon, I think, that will be all we have and, without wanting to make Ada Doom of myself, I swear this great oath: if the hare *does* disappear from our countryside, we are doomed. It is too important a chain in the links that bind us together and keep us alive to disappear without affecting us all. The hare is an archetype, one of the original symbols that man has used to make peace or come to terms with and explain his mysterious and often frightening environment. It has a place in myth and in story all over the world from the beginnings of memory. In a thirteenth-century poem from the Welsh borders, written as a ritual to be recited by the hunter on encountering a hare, there are seventy-seven names for the hare, including: the way-beater, the white-spotted one, the lurker in ditches, the filthy beast, the scutter, the fellow in the dew, the grass nibbler, old Goibert, the one who doesn't go straight home, the friendless one, the stag of the stubble, the cat of the wood ...

In China, they talk about the hare in the moon, not the man in the moon; in India, Egypt, Africa, the hare is a symbol of potency; the Native American Indians had the Great Hare of the Algonquin and, in Europe, there was a cult of the hare goddess, which is perhaps the origin of the association of hares and witches.

Hares are the most magic of creatures. It is not just about superstition and folklore, this magic associated with the hare; it is about the old role of animals as links between man and his gods, through dreams, through worship, through symbol. They are celebrated, vilified, revered and hated, feared and looked on with respect. I have always been filled with awe and horror at the idea of killing them and, at home in Ardboe, when I meet the man who I know kills them on the aerodrome, I will turn back before I will pass him. If I could, I would not have him live in the same parish. Such men carry with them the true odour of bad luck and ill omen. This superstition of mine goes back not just to the regard I have for the enchanted, wonderful animals I saw as I grew up beside that vast, unwanted aerodrome where, on the unhedged prairies between the runways that once sheltered small farms, the hares coursed and gambolled; not just back to the fact that behind me as I walked the aerodrome came a man who trapped every hare he could find, trapped them most cruelly so that, as they died slowly, they screamed, as hares do, like a woman or a baby. Then he brought parts of his horrible booty into Cookstown where the tax-payer paid him for every animal he slaughtered. No, it goes back to something far more atavistic, back to prehistory and our collective unconscious, back to our wonder at the hare's strange behaviour and strange appearances, back to what unites us in dread and in joy, back to when we believed in sacrifices and woodland deities, back to immemorial symbols, to beliefs buried so deeply in the unconscious of the human race that now we shy away from the knowledge, decry it or disallow it, anything rather than know again how powerful myth is in our lives and how, by avoiding it, we are disturbing the planet we live on. The hare in its seasonal abandon and appearances is the stuff of dreams and nightmares. Many's the time I have seen men turn back, unable to continue their journey because a dead hare lay on their path and to cross it would mean bad luck and misfortune; a pregnant woman would break her heart if she saw one because she was afraid her child would be born with a hare lip.

They are enchanted creatures and I have found them enchanting ever since, as a child, I spent hours watching them not for the sake of it but because I was searching for larks' nests which were made in the same terrain as a hare made its form or shallow burrow. I was a good and careful child and tried not to disturb sleeping animals and nesting birds but the hare would uncrouch before I got near its form and watch me; that ovoid, umber shape would suddenly twist and leap and land many feet away in order to leave no scent from the paws, then it would bound long and high, spinning out across the field in a subtle curve to leave no constant line of scent. After it had got out of range, it would stop and sit bolt upright, its paws clasped in front reconnoitring, then off again. The ears would stay erect until the hare reached top speed when they would flatten back and she (I hate calling a hare *it*) was travelling at up to thirty-five miles an hour. The hare never took a short cut; she knew she might be up against a greyhound or lurcher who could outflank her; unlike the rabbit which scuttles towards the nearest covert, a hare will run with great force across the open field, feinting and swerving without losing speed. As she runs, she makes what are called 'pups', little marks and indentations where the pads hit the ground so that after she had gone, you could follow her course. In those days, I did not watch the hare run but would keep my eyes fixed on the place from which she had risen and, when I reached it, would lie down in the form. A hare lies with her back to the weather, sheltered by the best wall she can make or find and, as she so lies, the grass or the heather takes on her shape. I cannot describe to you, only a poet could, what it was like to feel the warmth left behind, electric, soft, sluttish, crackling with velocity and energy.

Lying there, I would watch the lark rise. We all know about the lark but who has seen it surging upwards? No matter how high it rises from that astounding vertical take-off, it never disappears. I would watch it drilling its way up into the azure transparency when its notes fell like glazed shavings of blue sound and bounced off my ear. I can hear them still. Wordsworth said he had been sprung into poetry by hearing the sound of a walnut dropping; such sounds are not heard by many people now and I was blessed to hear them. The year after I did my eleven-plus exam, it was over. I never heard nor saw nature like that again. The noble savage went to the convent school.

Now the hares are disappearing, harried out of existence. It used to be that, at Aldergrove airport on the shores of the lough, up to seventy or eighty hares would course alongside the aeroplane as it landed or took off; you wouldn't see such a sight now.

They are chased for sport, week in and week out. I listen to dick-heads talking about how a muzzle stops the cruelty and reflect that I have never met a person at a coursing meet or a hunt who wasn't a moral dunderhead. Some go so far as to tell you, solemnly, that animals enjoy being hunted. What planet do such people live on? If you were being chased through your house by a mad axe-man who, when he catches you, tells you the blade is blunt, I don't think you'd be a happy bunny. I watch those moral guardians of ours, priests, at coursing events, see their faces distended with pleasure at the cruelty and know that next Sunday they will have the neck to preach moral behaviour to their flock. For flock read sheep; and sheep are creatures to be fleeced, driven around the world piled on top of each other, suffocating, dying with thirst, until they are slaughtered.

I have no crazed desire to upset the institutions of the country. I have two hundred acres of land which ten years ago harboured the hare – the hopper of ditches, the cropper of corn, the wee brown cow, the pair of leather horns, the little leverets and their long-eared parents. Now there are none. We neither shoot, hunt nor use fertilisers; there are no tractors; we do not make silage; we farm as land was farmed a hundred years ago, cropping with the seasons, yet I have not seen a hare in three years. I share the animal emotions. I grieve. An organisation called Hare Watch in England reports they are disappearing fast; and why not? Not long ago a syndicate in West Suffolk shot eight thousand hares on an organised shoot. Some experts think that in certain parts of the country hares appear to have stopped breeding. Given up, I shouldn't wonder, traumatised out of existence. I won't let the hunt harass foxes to death on our land or close up their hides, so that when the exhausted and desperate animal gets to its haven, he finds it has been stopped up. No animal would do that to another animal. Yet at a dinner party, I have often found myself sitting next to someone who tells me with relish what anti-hunt people are really like and what he would like to do with them. I know he is a good hater and an angry, bored, frustrated, impotent man and that's partly what his lust to kill is about. I'm often too bored or too much of a coward to tell them I'm anti-hunt myself. I was in the West of Ireland last year when the newspapers published a photograph of the Queen holding a pheasant by its broken wing and clubbing it to death. Have you, reading this, ever looked at a pheasant? Its iridescent plumage, spectacular colours, sheer beauty? Have you ever seen a hen pheasant tending her young, clucking anxiously as they stagger across the field? And why was the Queen beating the bird to death? Well, my dears, to put it out of its misery. Oh, that's all right then. But why was it in misery, this exquisite wild creature? Silly me. Her husband had shot it, but not very accurately, so it was dying slowly. So she took out the little club she carries for such a purpose and, merciful as she is, beat it to death. The people I was supping with were furious; furious with the spies, the cameras and the media yobs who would embarrass the Queen like that. But she comes from good stock. Her grandfather shot over a hundred birds in a single day; on 5 February 1952 her father killed a hare at full speed. It is recorded that he especially enjoyed this last kill. A few hours later, he himself was dead.

One of the arguments put forward by those who get enjoyment from chasing animals to death is that dogs will naturally chase hares, that it is part of their nature. William Cowper, during one of his long periods of sanity (he suffered from manic depression), kept hares. They became his companions and hastened his recovery. He wrote most tenderly about them and kept them for ten years. 'There is no natural antipathy between dog and hare,' he wrote, 'the dog pursues because he is trained to it.' Cowper's hares and his dog 'ate bread at the same time out of the same hand and are in all respects sociable and friendly'.

The struggle towards animal rights is a long one and will be over only when our grandchildren are watching videos of how it used to be; hares in a meadow, badgers in a wood, all disappeared into nostalgia and heritage parks. We are all part of a living entity that is the earth; and we are going to have to stop treating other things on this planet as though they were objects for our use. We are killing them and in so doing, we are killing our poetry, our souls, our imagination and ourselves.

DUBLIN OPINION

She said, 'Mum? When someone in Dublin says they're not a bit annoyed, not in the least, does that mean they're very annoyed?'

'Who's been saying it?'

'It doesn't matter. I just wanted to know the meaning.'

'The meaning depends on who said it,' I said, 'when they said it, why they said it and if they were sober.'

'I dunno,' she said, 'but he seemed a bit annoyed before he fell over; what does "stocious" mean?'

'It means he was very cross indeed,' I said, 'and very drunk. Where were you when this happened?' I was the more curious because contrary to myth, manifestations of drunkenness in Dublin seem rarer than in London, say, although perhaps I lead a sheltered life here, offisher. I do remember after a match at Lansdowne, one far-gone man with Rastafarian locks climbing, contented enough, into my skip perhaps on the assumption that it was his bed or his car; I didn't enquire as to his thought processes but warned that it was not a good resting place, if only because my neighbour John might at any moment retrieve him from the skip and hoard him in the cellar without much noticing. John and I could vie about skips but I know he would always win; he is a more obdurate, elaborate, committed, obsessive hoarder than I am. I am dazzled by his retrieval skills; he is a maestro in the art of assemblage. He has even been known to salvage things out of my skip. Jeananne said the other day: 'I see John has sent Alix and the children away and has ordered a skip in their place – it won't last.'

Oh, Dubliners can be very droll.

This is my fourth skip. The man who delivers them is one of the most beautiful creatures I have ever clapped eyes on and has absolutely no idea of his own beauty. He puts on huge gloves to clamp the chains and hooks into the side of the skip, lowers the great erect pulley and lifts the whole big filled-up affair into the air – no wonder my little heart goes pit-a-pat. He is not the reason for the four skips but he helps break the tedium. How could this much rubbish come out of a small garden some thirty-five yards long and fifteen feet wide? This fourth skip is not by any means the last.

One of the things that distinguishes our age from an earlier age is the amount of rubbish we have and make and buy and throw away; over the centuries, my little front garden obviously became a depository for everything under the sun, as well as the Leisure Centre and Public Convenience for the local cats who are put out (to say the least) to find their territory taken over by black plastic bags, flowers, paving stones, cleaner-uppers and, worst of all, those she-creatures of the Devil, dogs. They cannot believe that dogs like mine are allowed to exist and are in residence Next Door. The cats, frustrated, slink along the new *stalag* fence, turning and twisting, dabbing at the wire mesh, determined to mark their boundary (aka my garden), especially one huge, scarred patriarch with a single greeny-yellow eye who puts me in mind of that poem which half-cut men would intone, tears in their eyes, in many's a pub of an evening: 'There's a one-eyed yellow idol to the north of Khatmandu ... there's a little marble cross below the town, there's a broken-hearted woman tends the grave of mad Carew and the Yellow God forever gazes down ...'

There's nothing this big, bad, green-eyed cat would like to see more than a little marble cross bearing the names of Pester and Kafka (which my dogs, formerly known as Loulou and Yum-Yum, have been re-christened as being better fitted to their characters). This huge, tawny, feral creaturecat and its partner I have rechristened Spoor and Spray, SS for short, and they teeter on the posts of the fence while Pester and Kafka keep constant vigil, willing these Don Corleones of the cat mafia, to fall, arse over tit, into our garden, so they can savage them to cruel, tattered death. They forget that, when the cats did once trapeze down to make their mark, the dogs were well-drubbed and came limping in, hair on end, noses bleeding, eyes popping, dribbling and yowling, to howl their defiance from the window. Watching them gibber and squeak, I pondered on how anyone can buy into the deal that dogs are clever and can suss out what we are saying. If they had even a modicum of brain they would surely have intuited, after living with us for tens of thousands of years, that we do not want their great paw marks all over our yellow silk upholstered sofas. Talk about dumb friends. That UR-woman in the grass skirt who screeched 'get off the bleedin' yak skin' has her descendant in me, but the dogs are still all over the furniture shaking themselves dry and paddling wetly and adroitly across a clean floor, wagging their tails at burglars with great, pleased grins on their goofy faces. Everyone warns me about the blatancy of Dublin 'burgulars', as they are called, their cheek and brazenness, but Pester and Kafka beckon any passing burglar on in.

I leave the cats and dogs, go for a walk and am peering at a lovely chair in a shop window in Lower Pembroke Street, when a small, sharp-faced, bespectacled man in the shop sees me admiring the chair and invites me to cross the mews to his wonderful workroom. I fall upon a tremendous, huge, elaborate gilt mirror, all harps and shamrocks but needing restoration, and he says, amused by my curiosity and covetousness, 'You can have it for £150,000.'

Perhaps not today, I say. Looking at his glinty, intelligent face, his assurance, his shyness, I was reminded of *Dublin Opinion*, the humorous magazine, which, when I was a child, gave me an idea of Dublin as the City of Laughter. It was a place populated by artful creatures, gamblers, would-be gents, dim-witted Anglo-Irish, all intent on holding their own against certain citizens, i.e., Dubliners, who would always get the better of them simply by being cleverer and wittier and more worldly.

This was a man from its pages and, within two minutes of conversation, I could see he was a perfectionist about furniture. So I told him about my Irish Regency sofa and its bad, mad legs and how I couldn't live with it any more. All I could see as soon as I opened the front door were its cabriole legs where they should be sabre. 'I can't live with it,' I cried.

'You must,' he said, unmoved.

'*You* could change them,' I said, all artful, 'to how they should be.'

'I could indeed,' he said, 'but I won't.'

I tried a different tack to lull him. 'Is that limewood that mirror is made out of?' He looked at me with more interest.

A voice behind said, 'It wouldn't be limewood; limewood is such a lovely wood it would never have been painted over.' It was the voice of authority, the Knight of Glin, one of the most knowledgeable men in all Ireland about Irish furniture and paintings, who'd come in to look at the mirror. We kissed, mmmm, mmmm, air kisses and the furniture man looked on fairly indulgently at such nonsense.

I said, 'I'm telling him about my sofa, how I can't live with it.'

'And I'm after telling her she has to,' he said.

'I can't,' I said. 'And I'm after telling him I can't.'

'She's right,' Desmond said. 'It's a mess. You go round, Tommy, and tell her what she's got to do to get it right.'

'The only problem,' I said, 'apart of course from the legs, is that it's beautifully upholstered.' I did not say the yellow watered silk had cost a fortune, even with getting it wholesale through my friend Judy, but they both knew the subtext.

'I wouldn't touch it if it's upholstered,' Tommy said.

'You might be able to save some of the upholstery,' Desmond said.

'I wouldn't guarantee anything,' he said, 'but anyway, I'll come round and see it on Monday, so.'

On the Saturday morning, I went to Michael Conlon, one of the best dealers in Dublin, and certainly the most laconic. Michael's furniture is not scratchable; shabby chic is not in it; it is scratched, scored and jagged, and often falling apart, but the point is that the furniture he finds with his fine eye has seen better days and will again. 'Don't go scratching any surfaces with your handbag,' he said. As I said, they can be very droll, Dubliners.

Then my new friend Tommy walked in. 'Ah, there's the sofa woman,' he said. 'She gets around.'

'She does,' Michael said.

'He's coming to look at that sofa,' I said.

Michael looked gloomy. 'The legs, the legs,' he said.

'I've heard tell,' Tommy said, 'and I have my doubts. I'm not promising anything but I'm having a look on Monday. Twelve noon.'

On Monday, I was redd up and so was the house, waiting for Mr Mitchell. The cats were stuck on the points of their posts, the dogs dribbled at the window. Twelve, one, one-fifteen, one-sixteen; no sign. And such a nice, precise man. I telephoned the shop and said in that irritated, righteous voice that only those who are themselves habitually late have at the ready, 'I believe Mr Mitchell had an appointment with me at twelve o'clock.'

There was an awful silence. The voice said, 'I'm sorry to have to tell you that Mr Mitchell died this morning.'

Time stands still at these moments and your priorities change. I sat on the sofa and grieved. I had known him for about a day altogether but I knew I had met a man of great quality.

Later the same day, Mort the carpenter came round to do the hundred horrid little jobs that seem to live in the corners of every house and creep out when you are not looking. Mort's full name is Mortimer, after the great Irish soldier, and it is perhaps the most exotic name of a Dublin man I have ever heard. Parents call their children Gary, Lorcan, Jason, even Orlando, for heaven's sake, or Feidhlimidh and Cúchulainn for all I know. (Incidentally Standish O'Grady said that if he had known how to pronounce Cúchulainn or had heard it said, he would have interpreted the Irish sagas in a different way. Apparently he pronounced it *Kikulane*. It comes of being called Standish. But then again my mother, all her life, when she wanted a sofa covered would set off for the *youfolsterers*. You can see the psychological significance of the yellow sofa now, surely?)

When Mort was marking out where to hang the smart new magnifying mirror (*why, why?* I hear you cry) and pulling it in and out, I saw him suddenly recoil.

'Maybe I should try it the other way round,' he said.

I held it in place for him as he pencilled in where the screws should go and, looking into its masochistic depths, saw an appalling, mad-eyed, hairy image zooming out at me. No wonder Mort recoiled. I've bought a mirror that makes anyone who looks into it look like Corleone, the cat next door.

It was pissing with rain, cats and dogs stuff, and cold. When I left Somerset the sun was splitting the trees, but in Dublin it was the coldest, wettest month on record.

'It used to be,' I said bitterly, 'you could depend on a bit of spring in May. Now you can't; the whole climate has changed.'

Mort said, 'It's supposed to all be down to the ...' he hesitated.

'The greenhouse effect?' I said.

'No, the Bible says ... the end of the world ... season will meet with season.' He smiled. 'I wouldn't mind,' he said, 'I'd rather we all went, all together.'

'I'd rather go out on my own,' I said, 'leaving people behind crazed with grief. But until then I wish I didn't have to go out at all, especially in this weather. Imagine that going to the shops for a pint of milk in May means you have to dress as if you were going on a fishing excursion in November.'

I spend so much of my time whining and moaning as a comforting sort of background noise that it never occurred to me that Mort was listening. As he was leaving, I suggested he borrow an umbrella and he looked downright alarmed. My dad was the same. Some atavistic memory of the first days of umbrella-users in Europe when they were stoned as Children of the Snail Devil. The Irish have long memories. I think it was Terence de Vere White, that lovely man, who said that, when an Irishman sees a leaking tap, his mind hops back to the Flood.

'It's going to be like this all day,' Mort said, 'so I'll make a run for it,' but he was soaked before he got to the bottom of the steps.

I went back to my interesting job of scratching the sticky label off a Chinese cabinet with a jagged fingernail. (Why will most antique dealers use them?) When creating an effect of Instant Heritage, sticky labels are not a Good Thing; indeed one might end up being like someone who bought all one's own furniture, a remark quoted by Alan Clark in his memoirs, about Michael Heseltine and surely one of the sublime moments of English snobbery.

The doorbell rang and Pester and Kafka hurled themselves out to where Mort, thoroughly soaked, was holding out a carton of milk. 'To save you going,' he said. 'No point in two of us getting wet.'

It could only happen in Dublin.

When the rain finally stopped, I went back round to Michael Conlon's where you never see a sticky label and bought two round granite balls, with carved straps. They were extremely large and heavy, and the men who delivered them were exhausted by the time they had rolled the balls into the garden. In the time lapse between the fourth and fifth skip, the balls became covered with more rubbish from the excavated garden. I asked the dustbinmen would they take the rubbish away (don't ask if money changed hands). I saw from my window that they were helpfully attempting to drag away the balls as well, so I flung open the casement like Barbara Frietchie and shouted, 'The balls, the balls, leave the balls, don't touch the balls.'

'Thank God for that,' a dustbinman shouted back, 'they're lovely balls, but they could do you a mischief.' An old lady was hurrying past. I remembered Bay's question: 'When someone in Dublin says they're not a bit annoyed, not in the least, does that mean they're very annoyed?' I wanted to show her what annoyed looked like, but by the time I found her, the old woman had hurried on out of sight, blessing herself as she went, the dustbinmen had gone and only the feline yellow idol sat on the fence post dreaming of two dead dogs and an empty garden.

THE QUALITY OF WOMEN

All my life, I have had the luck of knowing astonishing women. Besides the manifest pleasures of their company, I love the way their houses look, their concern with others, how, in their busy lives, they can find the time and energy to look after their friends. These women do much the same level of work as men, but their surroundings reveal a love of beauty and a care for their environment that I do not, as a rule, see in the lives and surroundings of their male counterparts.

The standard was set early of course since I grew up among women out of the ordinary. This is not mere and fond prejudice. Perhaps, as a result of this high benchmark, I gravitate towards magical women, hoping the magic will rub off. Not that it should any longer be called magic or intuition, or whatever words we have had to use for so long, to cloak the idea of women's power so that either it seems arbitrary and crazy or it operates on some other planet away from the masculine world, so as to say 'real' world.

When women get actual power, powerful things change. When a woman was appointed head of the secretive and hateable atomic power industry in the US, she revealed terrible secrets about experiments that took place after the war, about tests that exposed unknowing people to lethal radiation to test their reactions; secrets that also revealed the moral turpitude of scientists and statesmen of the era – all men as it happens; secrets that should have been exposed long before. No man in the forty years since those experiments had ever admitted such terrible things had happened. When the mayor of Liége was shot, a woman magistrate kept so doggedly on the path of the murderers that she uncovered a web of corruption, lies and scandal in the Belgian government. In Ireland, women are changing values and behaviour in public places and, as more women are successful in political life in all the countries in Western Europe, I have no doubt the practice and values of politics will change there too. 'No more antler locking across the floor,' as someone said.

The course of my life has been changed and enriched by extraordinary women, some famous, most not, but, wherever and how ever they live or lived, they heightened life into a vivid adventure. Brought up on the verbal pyrotechnics of my sisters and brother, I find it hard to be patient with slowness of wit and language. I do not get the same kick out of New York as I did when Diana Vreeland was alive and ruling her roost there; I do not want to go to Paris and not see the view from Suzanne Lowry's apartment while listening to observations on the French which give more of an insight than a week of reading long reports. I'd be sorry to be in London and not visit Carmen Callil in a house filled with the books that might never again have seen the light of day had it not been for her and Virago; and I do not want to go to Venice and not stay with Peggy Guggenheim. But I can't. She is dead and her house is now a museum. Quite unlike anyone else I ever met, she opened my eyes to a good deal more than the art on her walls.

She lived in what sophisticates called the only bungalow on the Grand Canal; I called it a palace, the remarkable white stone vine-covered Palazzo Venier dei Leoni, started in 1747 and left unfinished for lack of money. She bought it just after the war for less than $50,000 and it was a magical house with one of the largest gardens in Venice and perfect for housing her extraordinary art collection. She loved Venice more than any place on earth and she shared her love for it. I spent my honeymoon there in a room where the waters of the Grand Canal lapped just below the windows; the bedhead was an Alexander Calder sculpture and a wonderful Picasso hung opposite the bed. Her remarkable drawingroom was crammed with pieces by Arp, Elsie de Wolfe white furniture, books and, of course, those extraordinary paintings and sculptures – a cull of treasures of the art of the first half of this century. Her taste had been formed by such diverse influences as her acquaintance with artists, her love for some of them, her involvement with artistic life all over the western world. She had luck on her side. She always insisted she was poor, but wealth is a relative thing and in the thirties she could buy more or less what she wanted. Her knowledge, flair and especially the timing of the forming of the collection made it unique.

Her stormy relationship with Jackson Pollock has been well documented. Basically, she put him under contract, tried to instil some kind of discipline into his life and undertook to buy and sell his paintings; all the same, she is sometimes represented as an exploiter of the tortured artist.

There were other aesthetic bonuses in staying with her – not least in setting out in her gondola (one of the last private gondolas in Venice) decorated with carvings of her little dogs, the gondolier wearing brass armbands by Max Ernst. When we sat on the terrace to watch the spectacle of Venice *en prince*, Peggy would sometimes unscrew the remarkable penis from Marino Marini's sculpture of a man on a horse, so as not to offend, she said, the sensibilities of a passing nun; the nun, it seemed to me, could only have been swimming by, since the terrace gave directly onto the water.

I was first introduced to Peggy in Venice in 1968 by my husband, and my first sighting of her was as she turned a corner in a street near the Zattere by San Gregorio, diagonally across the Grand Canal from St Mark's Square. There are more little streets and less canals in this area and, over the years, I came to know her distinctive silhouette outlined at the end of a dark *calle* followed by a flurry of small dogs, Shit'zus and Lhasa terriers, those little Tibetan shepherd dogs that tumble around like thistledown and look somewhat like the charming dogs in the beautiful Carpaccios, which are among the greatest treasures of Venice.

She walked like a dancer, toes turned out, elegant, careless, in vividly coloured mules which she had made and which were the only footwear I ever saw her wear except in England and New York where she wore boots. She was an addict of life, seemed to have a higher level of adrenalin and curiosity and excitement in her blood than anyone else and, wherever she was, she created excitement and disturbance because of this vivid life force. She was not in any conventional sense a generous person but she delivered extraordinary experiences. One starry midnight, she piled us all into her boat to cross the silent lagoon to the ancient cathedral at Torcello. Ruskin's words about Venice being a ghost with nothing but her loveliness to protect her were never so true as that ravishing night.

She was sexy, with bird-like bones, fantastic legs and a face dominated by an extraordinary squashy-tipped nose, the creation of a plastic surgeon in Cincinnati in the early days of plastic surgery. Her account of the operation and its result is typical in its insouciance and whim. 'I was bored. I could think of nothing better to do than to have it changed. It was ugly before but, after the operation, it was worse. I always knew when it was going to rain because my nose became a sort of barometer and would swell up in bad weather.'

When she was eleven, she fell passionately in love with her Irish riding teacher and continued to fall in and out of love for years and years ... When she decided to have an affair with Max Ernst (who, incidentally, she rescued from France at the beginning of the war), he, somewhat bewildered by her advances, asked, 'When, where and why shall I meet you?'

'Tomorrow, at four, in the Café de la Paix, and you know why.' She had known the way to Bohemia ever since the early twenties when she came to Paris to find a romantic alternative to her life as a poorer member of one of New York's richest Jewish families. (One of the galleries she opened in the course of her life was called Guggenheim Jeune, an ironic title to distinguish it from the world-famous Guggenheim Museum in New York, built by her uncle and which she was wont to refer to as 'The Garage'.)

In the sixties, she finally allowed her collection to be shown in her uncle's museum. By one of those extraordinary sequences of related events, the house we lived in on East 88th Street adjoined the Guggenheim Museum and, when she came for the opening of the exhibition, she stayed with us; and she would bang on her bedroom wall every night to let her pictures know she was near. She was never in the least surprised by coincidences like these, they had happened to her all her life. One memorable night, late, after dinner we slipped through a service side-door into the museum for a private view of her collection in its new unfamiliar setting, and there, highlighted by a single spotlight, shining into the surrounding circular darkness was Brancusi's great sculpture 'Bird in Space'. For years she had coveted it, had haggled over it, and in 1940 had finally acquired it, just as she fled Paris.

When she returned to Venice after the show in New York and before her paintings were sent back, she wrote to me: 'The house here looks so empty after your neighbour, so full of my children.' Referring to the pictures as her children was not merely sentimental. She felt they were her connection not only with the future and posterity, but also with her idea of herself.

She once gave me a shabby copy of her autobiography, *Out of this Century – Confessions of an Art Addict* (first published in 1946), which had long been out of print, and said that legend had that it the rest of her Guggenheim family was so scandalised by its uninhibited openness that they had bought up all the available copies and burnt them. (There is a new edition now.)

She had an indomitable spirit that I saw let her down only once. In 1979, after a foul operation on her eyes, she came to stay with us in England and, one tired and pain-filled night, she said she wished she were dead. The next day she came downstairs in purple dress and purple tights. 'I wish I hadn't said what I said. I never have talked like that and I don't want to start now. I've never suffered from self pity.'

Day after day, I listened to her talking and never wrote down a word, not even when she talked about Samuel Beckett, who she nicknamed Oblomov after a character in a Russian novel. I do remember her saying that, after she met him, they stayed in bed for four days and sent out for sandwiches to sustain them.

Last year, with my daughter, who was her god-daughter, I went to the Venice Biennale and, as we walked along the little streets towards the house, I felt I would see that silhouette, hear the click of the turquoise mules, see the tumble of dogs turn from the light into the dark; but those intricately wrought iron gates, studded with fat, coloured glass globules and rocks made for her by Clare Falkenstein ('Clare's knitting'), were tightly closed – a function for an AIDs charity was being held and we could not be let in.

THANK YOU FOR YOUR CUSTOM

She was off to Paris the next morning on a school trip and she was walking up the stairs well ahead of me. I was going after her, like a terrier after a bone, because I knew she'd borrowed my hairbrush, the only one that works on my hair, and she was denying it but laughing in that way that means, 'I'm lying, Mum, but so what'. I love her and her nose ring and her vocabulary. When someone behaves really, really badly, so that I'm speechless at their manners, she says sweetly, 'That was well rude', and I am calmed. She discovers three pieces of rotting chicken that Flossie, the neurotic Yorkie, has buried in her room against some famine day and, as the smell hits her, she says amiably, 'Rrrank out'. I know a whole code of words and ciphers to do with her generation, but they change all the time rather like the music she listens to, mooning, round-eyed, ears clamped with wires like something out of a fifties sci-fi movie and, where she used to follow me home, now I'm always a step behind her.

She was turning at the top of the stairs, foot poised for escape when I saw an odd flash. She moved. I saw it again.

'What's that on the soles of your feet?' Graceland lives.

'Nothing,' she said. The only time she says 'nothing' is when it's something in spades.

The house is rocking, the roof is lifting because she has forty friends raving away in her room. 'What are you doing up there?'

'Nothing.'

She has dropped a tray with six glasses, four tin plates and a steel bucket. 'What fell?'

'Nothing.'

So naturally I made her show me the 'nothing' on her feet. There were two huge holes in the soles of her shoes. You could see the calluses on her skin through them. I was horrified. No mother who is even half-way at home in her head ever supposes that a child, any child, will mention that a garment, shoe, object, needs mending. Maintenance in a family is sheer luck, intuition and a pathetic, gallant attempt to make and keep appointments. You fix up the dental appointment a month from today, the earliest he can fit you in, and you always remember on the evening of the day you were meant to go. So I knew that there was no point to scolding – not that that's ever stopped me – but what did puzzle me was why she was wearing these boots at all, since I knew she'd bought new ones in a smart shop just two weeks before.

'Why aren't you wearing the new ones?' I cried, starting back.

She looked shifty. 'They're not comfortable.'

'You're not proposing to wear those to Paris?' I asked, pointing at her feet. Rhetoric becomes a weapon in families. 'You couldn't. You walk miles in Paris and you'll do your feet a terrible injury. What's wrong with the new ones?' I was getting quite excited.

'OK. I'll take the new ones to Paris,' she said. It was her fast capitulation that made me nervy, suspicious. Normally it's skirmishes in the foothills and bodies on the mountain before she gives in.

'Well then, why aren't you wearing them now?'

'I like these ones. They fit my feet.'

'But they're ruining them.'

'My feet are used to them. They're hard where the holes are.'

'But you paid a fortune for those boots – show me them.'

'Oh Mum.' It's the long, drawn-out wail of true despair. I know I've hit pay dirt. There is something wrong with the boots and she doesn't want me to know because she thinks, quite rightly, that I will make a fuss. We find the boots in her room. That one sentence could be expanded into a few thousand words prose poem on how we found them, where we found them, under what we found them. There's a lovely poem by Theodore Roethke that springs to mind when I creep into her room and do a cull. 'I study the lines on a leaf: the little sleepers, numb nudgers in cold dimension, beetles in caves, newts, stone-deaf fishes.' Not that she's a zoologist, you understand: this is just how her room looks.

I stared at the boots, with real rising anger at the duds she'd been sold. Both heel mounts had collapsed so that she couldn't even begin to get her feet in. She had saved for months, she had worn them three or four times and they were utterly useless.

'We'll bring them back,' I said. 'This is a reputable company. Have you got your receipt?' I knew the answer very well. Did you ever keep a receipt in your life before you were about one hundred years old? My heart sank. I could rehearse the scenario: the bland faces of the salespeople; their refusal to take the boots back without a receipt, even though they were manifestly almost new, soles unscuffed, their brand name blazoned all over the insteps. I couldn't face it, so I phoned their head office and explained the situation. The woman there professed surprise that I might anticipate trouble. I said it wasn't always sweetness and light in their branches without a receipt and asked her to ring the branch herself, but she said she could guarantee I should have no trouble. So I cleaned myself up nice, found, Oh joy! the original boot bag, routed out my daughter from the back of her cave and, eyes glittering, set out.

A big, dark shop it was, in a chic street, with glorious shoes in the window. Inside a few women were trying on shoes or staring hopelessly ahead, waiting for service, and, at the back, on a kind of large dais, where stood the gleaming counter and the paraphernalia of the computers and pay machines, a group of women watched us approach. As I got closer, I tried to suss out who had the most sympathetic body language, but it was like gauging which of the harpies would soften first. (You will recall that the harpies are a representation of the evil harmonies of cosmic energies.) I knew my daughter, hovering near my shoulder, was anxious that I shouldn't, at all costs, make a scene. It's odd that almost the worst possible scenario for your children is to say to anyone anything that isn't utterly placatory and mild. 'Oh dear, look – you've banged into my car, but never mind,' is the ideal reaction when some lunatic has pranged you from behind and your children are with you and watching you like goblins.

I explained to the nearest saleswoman about my call to head office, blah, blah, blah, and, to my surprise, she said she'd give me a refund; at which point one of the other harpies said she should check with the manager. My heart sank. When he came nosing and blinking his way out of his little nest at the back, it sank even further; a sandy, ferrety creature he was, with sharp teeth showing in a sharp smile and, when I saw him, I comprehended I had already lost. This was neither a magnanimous nor a helpful man, and I knew him, as my dad would say, like a begging ass. Mr Jobsworth himself, the one who gets his jollies from being unhelpful, who wields his tiny, miserly piece of power triumphantly, as though that could make him potent.

I explained my case. He stared at me, enjoying it, enjoying my discomfort, my daughter's unease, enjoying the attention of the hench-woman. He looked at the boots, almost unmarked save for the name of his organisation, totally unwearable. He side-stepped the issue of the receipt completely. 'I'll have to send them back to the factory for analysis, madam,' he said.

'Well do,' I said. 'But my daughter is going away tomorrow and needs replacement boots today.'

'I don't think madam heard,' he said. 'They have to go back to the factory to see what's wrong.'

'But I'm not interested in what's wrong with your manufacture,' I said. 'Though I quite see why you are. We just need another pair of boots.'

'We can't give you another pair until we see what's wrong with these ones,' he said.

'But what does it matter what's wrong, to me, the customer?' I said, trying not to sound like Mrs Gummidge. 'You find out by all means, but we need the boots – which we've paid for.'

'I don't think madam is hearing what I said,' he repeated, pointing his little teeth at me. What did he think I was doing? Sitting like rhubarb under a bucket?

But I knew I was defeated. He wasn't going to give me replacements; the best thing was to leave with my dignity, cut my losses. So I said politely, in order to keep everything low key because something feral was happening in my body, 'Fine. As soon as you hear, can you send me a letter and a refund please?'

I put the boots on the counter; and, as he lifted them and bent down to take my name and address, he did a foolish thing. He smiled a sly little smile of triumph to the assistant who had summoned him from up from his lair.

Now I digress a little here to say that the Devlins were the Praetorian guard to the O'Neills, bred to fight, the Hatchet Men. One thousand of their small tribe fell in battle in the years of the Great O'Neill's campaigns. That old breeding lies quick in every Devlin's veins. Well, in every Irish person's. It lies dormant, like a bullet in an unfired gun. Touch the trigger and there's trouble, things go beyond control, not just on the move but hurling out. Fortunately, the trigger is quite hard to get at and fairly swaddled in restraints. But his smile, his meanness, his way of dealing with me, as no doubt he dealt with many of the women who gave him his living, didn't just touch the trigger, it pulled it hard.

I was at the counter before I knew I'd moved, and the first thing I lifted was the computer monitor screen. It was attached to cables and power points and, as I lifted and threw it, took a lot of debris in its wake. As it hit the display cases, its interior exploded. The women in the front of the shop, until then, as far as I knew, staring into the distance, waiting for service, got up and ran into the street.

The harpies began to scream, the manager shouted, 'The police, get the police!' So I lifted the phone and threw it at him. Then, still on the incandescent, dynamic energy that rage of this calamitous nature brings, I reached the credit card terminal and threw it to the other side of the shop, and finally, like Samson with the pillars, I pushed the cash register off the counter. It too was connected so it hung, piteous and screaming.

'Give me back the boots,' I said to the manager.

In a moment of spontaneous, ordinary emotion, such, I would hazard, as he hadn't allowed himself for years, his little watery eyes blazed and he threw – nay, hurled – the boots at me. I caught them, one in each hand, and my daughter and I walked out of the shop. She hadn't spoken a word.

I noticed from the Department of Employment posters, as I

drove home, that it was *Take Your Daughter to Work* day. As she walked up the stairs, she turned round. She was smiling. 'That was well rude, Mum,' she said. 'I should think you done his head in.'

READING LESSONS

D o you ever read or hear something and wish that you hadn't? I fear I'm going to share certain things with you which you may well wish I hadn't; so, as they say on the telly, you can now switch off. But who does? I try to. I don't go to films that portray violence, don't look at television programmes that peddle killings or cruelty, can no longer take the rough with the smooth. It means I can't discuss *The Silence of the Lambs* or *Reservoir Dogs* or *Seven*. A secondary benefit is that I don't give money to people who contribute to what critic I.A. Richards called the only calamity, the degradation of good.

This process of culling began a long time ago, oddly enough through that supposed haven – literature. There are passages and things in books and pictures I wish I'd never read. The story of the child dying as he cried in the woods in Adam Bede is one and, on a different plane of sentiment, another is 'The Old Fools' by Philip Larkin, a poem about you and me in a few years.

> What do you think has happened, the old fools:
> To make them like this? Do they somehow
> suppose

> It's more grown up when your mouth hangs open
>   and drools
> And you keep on pissing yourself and can't
>   remember
> Who called this morning?...

This is a bulletin from the future and thus perhaps avoidable; so would you rather our doctors and scientists went on researching so you don't piss and drool and forget the name of your own children? In that case you will have few qualms about reading this next, on what we do to keep young and healthy. By the same poet, it's called 'The Ape Experiment Room':

> Buried among white rooms
> Whose lights in clusters beam
> Like suddenly-caused pain
> And where behind rows of mesh
> Uneasy shifting resumes
> As sterilisers steam

If you can read that without shifting uneasily, without your flesh crawling, then you've been watching too much television or something; certainly the carapace we all need has hardened to implacable.

    Then there's 'Aubade' in which Larkin sees clearly, as clearly as Beckett ever did, what lies ahead, the dark room where we forfeit memory and no longer hear or see our sisters and friends and those who had beauty and wit and smiled ...

> This is what we fear – no sight, no sound,
> No touch, or taste or smell, nothing to think with
> Nothing to love or link with
> The anaesthetic from which none come round.

Reading contributed to my loss of innocence, though I suspect that innocence, like truth, is indivisible; certainly reading underwrote the moment when, as a child, I watched innocence flee my life; this is no piece of sophistry. I remember it as clearly as I remember the day I had fourteen stitches sewn clumsily into my leg by Dr Brown in Coagh.

The first time I ever knew I could read something and wish I hadn't was in *Jude the Obscure*. Until then (I suppose I was about thirteen), it never occurred to me that an image could be implanted that I wouldn't want or couldn't shake out. God knows they were innocent times. Today there is hardly an hour passes but there's an image on the telly, a picture in the newspaper, a sound-bite you wish you hadn't heard; that you want to shake violently from your soul-bank. In *Jude the Obscure* what happens is so horrible, so terrible you can't begin to believe it, even though Hardy leads you up to it. Sue, the heroine (though she is not, she is a woman like all of us and heroines tend to be token women), complains of her despair, weeps about her plight to her small son and answers his simple but probing questions about himself and his brother and sister. Sue leaves the house and, on her return, has difficulty pushing open the door of the bedroom where Jude and she have left the children. Jude hears her shriek and hastens forward into the room but there is no sign of them.

He looked in bewilderment round the room. At the back of the door were fixed two hooks for hanging garments, and from these the forms of the two youngest children were suspended, by a piece of box-cord round each of their necks, while from a nail a few yards off, the body of little Jude was hanging in a similar manner.

On the floor lay a piece of paper on which was written in the boy's hand, 'Done because we are too menny.'

Once I read that, there was no going back to the world of fairy tales. Another horrible moment in literature occurs in Dostoevsky's memoirs, *The House of the Dead*. He is not a laugh a minute at the best of times and the things that happened to this tender-hearted man hardly bear repeating. While in prison for his political beliefs, he was thrown in with the lowest and most vile criminals. He befriended Sharik, a dog that somehow survived in the prison, scavenging, hungry, loving. The love of this dog, paradoxically, kept Dostoevsky in touch with humanity. To his horror he found out that the other prisoners stole dogs, which they skinned and used to make boots. One day, he saw the prisoners with a magnificent, large black dog 'evidently of an expensive breed. Some good for nothing manservant had stolen it from his master and sold it to our shoe makers. The poor animal seemed to understand the fate in store for it. It looked searchingly and uneasily from one to another of us there and occasionally ventured on, a slight wave of a bushy tail hanging between its legs, as if trying to soften our hearts by this sign of trust in us ...'

That tail wagging is what makes this passage so dreadful to me. Dogs have done something so extraordinary in breaking through the prophetic circle, in leaving their own animal nature to come bounding towards us. And how do we treat these extraordinary creatures which have thrown in their lot with us? Go to any rescue centre or animal hospital and you will see. The point about most of these passages is that I genuinely wish I hadn't read them. Not because I wish to block off from cruelty and danger, but because in all the passages there is a reiteration of something I know too well, the heartlessness of man and his tragedies. In them I am told, by peerless writers, something of the world's sadness and of its cruelties I already know and try to keep at bay. Such incontestable passages knock down my defences, which are too fragile and too hard to re-erect for me to be sanguine about them being tampered with. I am prone to depressions that leave me ill and incapacitated and such things can trigger them; so why am I loading them onto you, I hear you cry. Dunno. Perhaps I feel by communicating them, I am taking them back into the light and they won't fester any more in my head. I won't mention heart.

So it's the things I know that are verified by these writers that make me so sad – reading them makes me realise my own fears are not singular horrid fantasies but endlessly realised.

> The hare we had run over
> Bounced about the road
> On the springing curve
> Of its spine.

That bounce of death in Norman MacCaig's poem is remembered by me every day as I walk the fields, the empty fields. Only a poet could have conveyed its desolation. 'We broke the hare's neck and made that place, for a moment the most important place there was.' The hare has jumped in death into its future, as part of my bitter and outraged memories, laid down when, years ago, I heard hares being killed in Ardboe. 'In order to climb into the depths,' wrote Wittgenstein, 'one does not need to travel very far. No, for that you do not need to abandon your immediate and accustomed environment.'

When my children were babies, for about a year after each birth, I had to have the newspapers censored – rather, I should say, the papers were censored for me and I would find large scissored holes on every page, like somebody living in a totalitarian state. These holes were where my husband and those around me who cared for me had cut out the increasing number of stories about cruelty to children. I had long since ceased to watch or listen to the news. There was a spate of news stories about cruelty to babies and children around that time, stories that still fester away, foul and dark, their shapes moving under the surface of our lives. Maria Colwell starved to death, Zoe, battered, John burned and tortured. For all the censoring, still I knew about these children and lived in a state of grief and terror. Now, I know that the biological instinct to protect at all costs that which is vulnerable and one's own, over-rides all else and anything that threatens it is monumentally dangerous. Many women suffer from this same terror and sensibility when their babies are young. This fierce instinctive response is something we share with all animals, and one of the reasons I am a vegetarian is because of hearing cattle lowing in pain and sheep crying when their lambs are taken away from them. And one of the reasons I stopped believing in religion was because, as a young girl, I read Pope Pius XII's ringing statement – an endorsement of Descartes' view – that animals did not feel pain. Pius XII proclaimed that cries from an abattoir should not arouse compassion or anger any more than 'do red hot metal undergoing the blow of the hammer'. Both these men were unobservant and unfeeling – whatever else they might have been – and, what's more, they were badly damaged and emotionally stunted people. Yet for years their views prevailed and Pius XII was revered, though, from all I read of him, he had a stunted heart.

Gaining this kind of unrebuttable knowledge is quite different from having your conscience stirred. That I can always do with. Here is conscience-prodding by that master of the art, W.H. Auden, written in 1938:

> And gentle do not care to know
> Where Poland draws her Eastern bow,
> What violence is done;
> Nor ask what doubtful act allows
> Our freedom in this Irish house,
> Our picnics in the sun.

Actually, he wrote 'English house', but it applies wherever. I think of Bosnia and Srebrenica and I think of some of the most beautiful summers I ever spent in Dublin and in Somerset in a parallel time. Whenever I read great poetic truths, as in any of these passages, they are so unforgivably unforgettable they make me mad. I always thought Larkin's pessimism, for example, so reliable, so ample and dark, took you so far into its dark embrace that its inconsolability could not be gainsaid. He delivered the body blows with such incontestable conviction especially as he had, underlying his despair, such a wonderful gallows humour. But recently I read another poet, with more courage and generosity and a wider heart, who looked at 'Aubade' and rescued me, the reader, in a way I could credit and trust.

Here's Larkin again:

> Courage is no good.
> It means not scaring others. Being brave,
> Lets no one off the grave.
> Death is no different whined at than withstood.'

So. Larkin at his bottomed-out, bottled-out best. All my tendencies to pessimism and timidity underwritten with authority. Nowhere to turn. Then in comes Heaney and stands at the door of the poetic room, holds it open and lets in the light. He shows that courage isn't a word, it's a duty and a virtue. Of 'Aubade', he says the poet does not hold up the lyre in the face of the gods of the underworld; the poem does not make the Orphic effort to haul life back up the slopes against all the odds. For all its heart-breaking truths and beauties, the poem reneges on what Yeats called the 'spiritual intellect's great work'. After I'd read that in *The Redress of Poetry* – the openness of it, the way he refuses to be cowed from using grand imagery by the degradation of words and their use in the last part of the twentieth century – I knew I was reading the most poetic way of naming depression I'm ever likely to read again. And I saw that, because Larkin was depressed, his vision must not necessarily be believed or shared since it is not necessarily true, his multiplicity of response has been scorified into bitterness and grief.

I remembered a passage I had read years and years ago when I set out on the voyage to try to become an artist. I typed it out on an incongruous square *Vogue* postcard with the *Vogue* telephone number at that time (still using letters GRO 9080) and pinned it up in my office. *Vogue* and the message made a fine collision:

> The book of unknown signs within me no-one could help me read by any rule, for its reading consists in an act of creation in which no-one can take our place and in which no-one can collaborate. And how many turn away from writing it, how many tasks will one not assume to avoid that one? But excuses do not count. The artist must at all times follow his instinct which makes art the most real thing, the most austere school in life and the last true judgement.

I've spent a good many years avoiding what Proust said. Now I hand it on to you to gnaw at your soul.

When my daughter was small, she asked me, 'Is there something you can do when you have cried too much, some new word? Is there an overcry?'

I don't know how I answered her then. *Now* I'd say, 'Yes. It's called "Hope".'

And in that way you make philosophy fit the facts and the facts fit the philosophy; the moment after I had read Seamus Heaney's lines, his request that we be hopeful in the face of despair, I remembered some lines from one of Larkin's greatest poems, 'The Trees':

> Yet still the unresting castles thresh
> In full grown thickness every May
> Last year is dead, they seem to say
> Begin afresh afresh afresh afresh.

You could almost think on a quick reading that Larkin was giving us hope; he both is and isn't – as was his wont (nobody can give such joy with one hand and such irredeemable blackness with the other). So my philosophy here is that I must over-ride that weasel verb, 'seems', and indeed begin afresh afresh afresh.

CHRISTMAS MIRACLE

I know what I'm getting for Christmas because I've already got it and it was born a thug and will die a thug. Standing about three inches off the ground, it is bat-eared, looks a little like a tiny Chinese pagoda, and, if it has a mind to, responds to the name Loulou. It is my fourth dog – I mean I have four all at the same time. Don't even ask. My husband, God love him, says the only reason he married me was that I didn't like dogs. And now that even this reason is gone, he can't get away. I've trained Mona, the bull terrier, to tackle and pin him down if he makes even the slightest dash for freedom.

My third dog Flossie, lugubrious and pessimistic as befits a dog from Yorkshire, reminds me of the Yorkshire man who, when asked how he had enjoyed the sights of Blackpool, said, 'It were all reet if tha' likes laughin'.' And what about Yum-Yum? I hear you cry. She has one eye and a broken tail and indeed I sometimes think if you melted all four dogs down and made one out of the result, you might get one complete dog. Might.

But all of this is mere preliminary to the Christmas miracle that happened to me and Loulou; it is also, I am sorry to say, tabloid testimony to a saint's sleaze. Indeed, St Anthony could be a member of the last Conservative government without any bother on him. The manifestation of the miracle started simply enough, on an ordinary day a week before Christmas.

I drove up Kensington Church Street, found a parking space (a miracle in itself) and took the dogs for a walk in the park. I don't know if you know but, in the Royal Parks of London, you watch your dogs all the time and when they answer to the squawk of nature, you scoop up their little offerings in a shameful bag and put it in the dog litter box. God knows what you do if you have a couple of Alsatians. Hire a dump truck I should think. And don't think you would not scoop the poop. There are vigilantes behind every tree, ready to jump out and point an accusing finger at you and the little dog mound.

So, after the dogs had pretended to kill all the squirrels, and I had avoided seeing what they were doing at the base of trees, we all got back in the car and drove down to Kensington High Street. I give you the geography so you may know I'm talking busy – one of the busiest streets in London – jammed with thousands of people and cars. I parked, fed the meter and legged it up to Marks, picked up the goods, and back. On the way, I met Lorenza, weary after her day's work, carrying bags. 'I'll give you a lift,' I said and, when we reached the car and the dogs began screaming and yelling and hurling abuse in the way they apparently must when they see any mortal being approaching the car doors, I told her to just sit down hard on all three – they soon get out of the way, except Loulou who's like a mushroom and can push her way up through flagstones. So Lorenza sat and as she did, said casually, 'Not as bad as usual; only two today.'

'No, three,' I said, 'there's three; I left Mona at home, but the others are all in here somewhere – Loulou, Yum-Yum, Flossie.'

'Polly,' she said, 'there are two dogs in the car.'

My heart stopped. 'Loulou?' I said. And then, my voice rising, 'Loulou?' She wasn't in the car. Six months old, a bundle of black and white, loving idiotic fun, greeting everyone with a huge smile, endearing, ridiculous, with no idea about traffic and no name tag on her collar (she's never out of my sight), no idea about anything and she's not in the car. It meant that, if she had hopped out without me noticing when I fed the meter, then she'd be wandering lost in one of the busiest, most dangerous streets in London, bar none, for over an hour.

At first I didn't panic or, more accurately, my panic was so deep I was frozen into calm. Now I must say here that, if you are neither a dog owner nor a dog lover, you won't understand my terror. If you are, you will.

I started to search but it was hopeless and, after a while, I too became hopeless. A thousand cars, a thousand people, a maze of streets, half dark. People hurrying and nowhere for a little dog, never before separated from friends and family, to go for refuge. As I called and searched, getting more desperate, the bustling crowds and anonymous faces separated into individual kind people who stopped in their juggernaut hurryings and helped in the search. The English really do love dogs. I gave up looking and ran to the police station where a queue of people waited, docile, miserable with documents and sorry tales to tell, and one hard-faced harassed officer behind the counter.

'My dog,' I said, from the end of the queue, 'my dog.' The line parted, the queue became anxious and sympathetic, the officer's face softened and without delay the particulars were on the computer. All the same, she didn't hold out much hope. By now all I could think was that if Loulou did survive, she would never again hear her own name. Even if whoever found her was good and caring, they wouldn't know what she was called.

I left the police station and began searching the streets again. I went back up towards the park but it was shut and the Palace windows were dark. As I hunted, some atavistic urge rose in my breast and I invoked the spirits of my childhood, imploring St Anthony in words I hadn't said in, oh, maybe thirty years. And I remembered, in some hidden recess of my mind or perhaps my soul, my mother declaring that St Anthony was the greatest capitalist in heaven and the easiest to buy. 'Promise him money,' she said, 'and he's yours.' So I must suppose that I prayed although it sounded to me curiously like a bribe.

I hunted on and finally, hope gone, began my miserable drive home. The other two dogs knew something was wrong and Yum-Yum huddled in the back seat. Flossie, of course, was in high good spirits. Life was just to her taste.

I took a different route home and there on Holland Park Avenue, picked out in the lights of the car, stood a tall man, isolated, on the side of the street, the rush hour traffic almost brushing him and in his arms, Loulou …

I stopped the car and he mouthed across the distance, 'Is she yours?'

I put my head on the steering wheel and began to cry.

He opened the car door. 'I can see she is,' he said. 'I saw her in road and thought yon's a loved dog. I reckoned someone would be back, looking for her, no doubt breaking their heart an' I were right.'

Loulou climbed onto my lap. Except for her little tongue licking my hand, she seemed as rigid as I had been when I first knew she was missing. 'She hasn't moved a muscle since I picked her up,' he said. 'And mind, she weren't an easy dog to pick up. She were right frightened. And there were a lady who wanted to take her home. She reckoned she was an abandoned dog. But I knew the dog were lost. I've always been a dog man myself.'

Where do you start asking a man about what motivates him to stand for three hours in the same blessed spot on a busy street in a city where no-one cares about their neighbour, to wait and wait as the evening lengthens and darkens because he reckons the owner of a small frightened lost dog is out there somewhere, searching and calling? How do you start to thank him? You know you've come across a miracle and that the spirit of that other manger – not the one with the dog in it – but the one that makes Christmas what it is, still lives on.

You've met St Anthony in the flesh down-to-earth and what's so marvellous is that he's so down-to-earth easy to thank. You keep your side of the bargain as he has kept his and you simply pay up. The parish priest is still smiling and so, dear reader, am I. So – A Happy Christmas from Loulou and me and Mona and Yum-Yum. Flossie says: No Comment.

THE WISHING TREE

If I had a wish, and a wish, if it is to be of any use, must be extravagant, impossible, beyond dreams. What's the use of wishing to win the lottery? – you might do that anyway. If I had a wish then, it would be that I could come back in sixty years, just for a little while, on a fine day and walk under my trees instead of walking over them. Five years ago, we planted five thousand oak saplings and I want to see them fully grown. To my mind, a mature oak is one of the most beautiful of all plants, in its dark verdant leaf, its crisp shape spreading so widely from its low boughs, not to mention the totally satisfactory feel and shape of an acorn. In sixty years, if the planet still exists – and increasingly, it seems as if it won't – my forest will look as it looks now in our dreams, a lost demesne.

Mind you, we do not live in the forest, it is for the future and I bear in mind Derek Mahon's stanza: 'I built my house / in a forest far / from the venal roar. / Somebody please / beat a path / to my door.' We are working to make something that should last for hundreds of years, I suppose I would rather write a great poem but since I can't, I will go along with Joyce Kilmer who thought he would never see a poem lovely as a tree. We are also doing it because if we don't, who will? Then there is the sheer joy and pleasure that come from doing something so palpable, so seeable. Perhaps there is something else. Kenneth Clark once wrote:

> There is a fear which seems to take possession of Western man every five hundred years, and as it is supposed to be connected with the millennium, it is known to historians as Chiliasm ... Can we escape from our fears by creating once again the image of an enclosed garden? It is a possible way of life: is it a possible basis for art? No. The artist may escape from battles and plagues but he cannot escape from an idea. The enclosed garden of the fifteenth century offered shelter from many terrors but it was based on a living idea, that nature was friendly and harmonious. Science has taught us that nature is the reverse; and we shall not recover our confidence in her until we have learnt or forgotten infinitely more than we know at present.

Chiliasm it may be, but we have found as we work on the land that Nature is benign, healing and harmonious. Every phase of this endeavour has not been unlike writing; draft after draft, trying to get it right, knowing the thing is there waiting to become alive in a shape made for it.

When we planted the first oaks in what was to be the oak forest, our fields looked as though they were memorials to dead fairies or fallen ballet dancers, certainly some cult or sect that only wore pink. (The man who invented these pink containers, which are in effect mini greenhouses, worked for a county council and never made a penny out of them; yet he is a great hero who has revolutionised tree planting. Without them our trees would be about ten inches high now; instead they are bursting up out of their seams. If he had patented his discovery, he would surely be a multi-millionaire, since they have been used ever since by every council, park planner and motorway planting company, indeed by everyone who plants trees in any quantity. The only drawback is their appearance, but that is temporary.) We have been restoring and planting for years and every so often we get another field, another stretch of dead land and the jigsaw gets more complete; we know the finished picture in our heads.

There is nothing that makes me rise up more than hearing someone say the best custodians of our land are farmers. Farmers behave like psychopaths towards the planet we all live on, part of which they are fortunate enough to own. Instead of cherishing, they wring it to death. They are greedy to the bone; they ruin the land; flatten features, over-harvest, nitrate it, cut the hedgerows, cut down trees and ill-treat their animals to get a penny more subsidy. They plough out landmarks, fill up dew ponds, spray wild flowers, mow in such a way the corncrake is practically extinct, the hare has nowhere to go and our children will never hear the lark. By the time they are finished, the land is bleeding dry and dead; it may look green to you but that green field is a nitrated desert. There are few farmers I know who could earn a living in any profession, but that will not stop them despising those who earn their living in other ways.

I grew up along the shores of Lough Neagh, a superb and unique merging of land and water. It is utterly changed. For an extra rood or two of land, the shore has been levelled, every boulder removed, the sally trees where the fishermen hung their nets cut down, the sedge, the rushes killed and where once the water and the land slid in a silky little rush towards each other in a fringe of grass and rushes and brown boulders, now there is a stiff line of virulent nitrated green, broken only where the deep rut of tractor has been driven to draw water for the cows that graze what was common territory. That lough shore, like our pasture here, lay like a palimpsest of a million years of continuous uninterrupted life. Gone, gone, gone.

All of our fields we bought from farmers and all, save one, had been ruined and that one I saved only by making Barbara Frietchie of myself, throwing my old grey head in front of the tractor to stop the farmer who had suddenly decided to spread nitrates and fertiliser on an old pasture; why was he doing it in such a hurry? Because he had heard the Nature Conservancy people were coming to have a look at it and he was going to nip that in the bud, heh. And why did he sell? Because I paid him well over the odds and he took me for a fool.

I wish I could describe this foolishness; it is a field of such beauty that people fall silent when they walk into it, suddenly aware, as was I when I first saw it, of what we have lost. Just as those we live with grow older so imperceptibly that we hardly notice the change, until suddenly we are confronted with an image out of our past and are forced into witnessing what has transpired, so older men and women who walk this meadow are the most moved; they stand silent, entranced, appalled, knee-deep in the tangled, pied thick beauty of the fields of their childhood, realising it has almost, elsewhere, vanished. This meadow which we hold in trust and have covenanted so it can never be ploughed (or, Orwell speak, 'improved') is now an SSSI, (a Site of Special Scientific Interest); a museum piece. The irony is that, until the EU, it was only one of tens of thousands of such fields in Somerset. Now there are only about ten fields left. It is a multi-coloured medieval tapestry or the background to a Botticelli painting, striped, flecked, spangled and eyed like a peacock. You wade through swards of purple and spotted orchids, brush past silverweed, devil's bit scabious, cornflowers, yellow vetchling, bird's foot trefoil, knapweed, ox-eye daisy, betony, cowslips, dyers, greenweed, timothy, sedges, vernal grass, rushes, horsetails, thistles, clovers, saxifrage, through eighty, yes, eighty, varieties growing in a prodigal muddle and realise that those great *mille fleur* tapestries of hounds and unicorns and ladies in their paradise of flowers were not a dream representation of some Utopia but an accurate account of what the artist saw around him. And the noise; a million flying butterflies, grasshoppers, ladybirds, moths and insects, whirring away like Kennedy airport of an evening.

Slowly we are bringing the other fields back to life. We use manure from organically fed animals. When we bought in manure it had to be kept at the side of a field for two years to lose its toxicity. God alone knows what effect the flesh of the unfortunate beasts from whom this poisoned manure came has had on those who eat it. Every year we gather the seed from the pasture field, till another field and spread the seed; every year more flowers grow; but I won't see the end results – my lifetime isn't long enough. But some child may, in the future.

Sometimes when I am in a rage about what has happened in my lifetime (avoiding the burnt-out zones of Hiroshima, the Holocaust), and think long on the disappearing hare, the almost extinct corncrake, the increasingly rare cuckoo, the silence of the larks, I calm myself by rehearsing what we are doing. Very little, but something; about the big things we can do nothing except remember daily. The small things have big statistics and when I recite them, an unholy peace descends. Five thousand trees, 1,800 tons of hard core, 1,000 tons of top soil, two dams (little dams, but dams), four JCBs (to restore the dew ponds the farmers ploughed over and to make paths through the forest that still lives in its little pink boxes). The JCBs wallow like yellow hippos, shifting mud around in the boggy little valleys, scooping out what I call lakes, my husband calls ponds and my daughters (whether to make peace or poke fun I can never tell) call *lakettes*. Three bridges, commissioned from Richard La Trobe Bateman, span these lakes. He started building bridges after he was asked to design a high table for an Oxford college; the problem was to make a table for all the Fellows (of whom there are a goodly number) and all their wives, without any one having to accommodate that table leg we have all been stuck between at formal dinners. When he had most elegantly solved the problem, he found he had in effect built a wonderful high bridge. Now the bridges he builds are a vibrant and certain mix of oak planks, wishful thinking and a slight edge of danger. The dogs run across them without thinking and I, too, confident, amble across and some day will fall in; first-timers take a deep breath and look around for Indiana Jones. These lakettes and bridges fringe the new forest in the centre of which stands an urn. More statistics, gentle readers. Carved 1740; twelve foot high; two tons in weight; sold out of a great garden by a vandal who should have known better but it was an ill wind. I now have healthy respect for people who build monuments on soil – the underpinnings are tremendous (just look at the Wellington Testimonial Obelisk in Phoenix Park – ninety-eight feet high, the largest in Europe and think how many feet under those foundations go).

Ours were slightly less deep, filled with cement, hard core and I don't know what else, and, one evening, I went down when the workmen had smoothed over almost the last layer of cement before the actual pedestals were laid; it was just hardening and irresistible and, with a pointy stick, I wrote: 'Andy and Polly caused this to be laid in October 1993'. When I went down the next day, the last layer of cement bore the legend 'Richard Gunston, mason, laid this in October 1993'. The urn stands high, baroque, magnificent, dominating the little trees in what one day will be an encircling oak grove ...

Perhaps by building an enclosed and enchanted garden, I cannot escape my fears but I can do what that great poet John Clare did nearly two hundred years ago – watch the rising of the lark, see the hawk hang in the summer sky, the kite take its circles round the wood, hear the wood pigeons clapping their wings among the dark oaks, hunt curious flowers in rapture and mutter thoughts in their praise. And I can ally myself with poets and artists in this work and say, post-Hiroshima, *I believe in the shadow of the oak.*

All the same, I would like to be granted my wish and just once on a sunny day, walk over the old fringed lakes down the paths under a canopy of leaves to find the urn in its hidden grove, its perfect proportions in perfect harmony with the spreading trees.

BOWER BIRD

*I*t's one of the most remarkable places in the world, the flea
market in Paris – that vast riddled acreage of stalls and shops,
arcades piled high with treasures and rubbish and hard-faced
women. I visit it every time I go there, usually before or after
having been to a museum. It's a salutary lesson going from one
form of conspicuous display to another. I went to it by Metro and,
as I was standing waiting on the platform for a change of train, I
was struck by two people talking, a little further up. The platform
was crowded but this couple, a man and a woman, I noticed for
two reasons: one, the intensity of their conversation – I couldn't
hear it – though I longed to, so passionate yet agreeably involved it
seemed and, secondly, I knew they were Irish or possibly Russian.
Certainly not French, Italian, German. How did I know? Any Irish
person knows. The tribal signals are all there. Not the markings –
one nation dresses much like another now, though the Italians are
generally well-groomed and *les petits soins* are a religion to the
French. No, it's the stance, the hands in the pocket, the tilt of the
head, the mobility of the face, the light in the eyes and of course, it

must be said in general, the total disregard for appearance. Only the Russians talk and stand the same way as the Irish and address each other with the same passionate one-to-one involvement.

Anyway I got on the train, two carriages down, very crowded but found a seat. One of the little tilt-down ones by the door and that was that. Then, to my surprise, I found the couple standing beside me. They had obviously moved down to the least full carriage, though it was still very crowded. The woman beside me got up to go and the Irish/Russian woman sat down. The man, who I took to be the husband, looked at me and said, 'Jesus, it's very hot.' We all three burst out laughing. They had obviously done the same tribal codifying with me. We talked in that immediate way I think only the Irish do and which always puts me in mind of something the great V.S. Pritchett observed in Dublin years ago, 'that the older people in the street look at you as though they must know who you are and who your people were'. (I digress here to say that a couple of months ago, walking up Castleblayney Main Street, I met an old, old man, a stranger who greeted me as we passed. 'Hello, daughter,' he said and I was suddenly so awash with tears that I had to stand still and grind my teeth to get control of myself. *Infantis dolor.*) Anyway, I had the same moment of something deep and tender being touched when the couple said they were from Clogherhead, and I remembered my mother talking of it as a place for delightful summer excursions from Drogheda when she was a young woman. They too had been to the Clignancourt *marché aux puces*, that astonishing conglomeration of stalls and shops where you can buy anything from a stuffed bear to a chandelier. I bought a totally necessary object – a striped silk palanquin, tasselled, fringed, gilded, plump silk cushions within, all of it like the tent Napoleon might have dreamed in, the night before battle. Standing twenty-four inches high, it is for a dog. If you discern a defiant note in this, remember I had to cart this object back to Ireland, pretending not to care, pretending not to blush. When the dogs saw it, they went all red and pushed behind each other so as not to be the first. They'd rather die. I also bought a small Irish chair.

One of the things that first got me interested in Irish furniture was when I read in a text book the dry little unemphatic sentence: 'There are no Irish vernacular coffers and cupboards before the mid-nineteenth century since the Irish had nothing to store.' It was a Damascene moment. I've not stopped collecting since. It's nice to be able to put a high moral gloss on an enjoyable but bad habit. Gambling, alcoholism, collecting, they are all related to a stifled creative urge as well as to other less romantic but no less painful things.

After the flea market, I walked to the Camondo Museum, measuring the Ardboe miles, both dreading and anticipating what I was going to see. I have been to this jewel of a house often before and will, if I'm spared, go again but always I am amazed by it. Now I hold (but then I would, wouldn't I) that making your own environment beautiful is as valid a work of art as any piece of writing, painting or any willed work; women do it all the time and get no formal credit for it. It's as though the handiwork, taste, inspiration and labour that go into composing a pretty room was happenstance.

The sad thing is that a beautiful interior is so ephemeral, so easily lost – even in families who have lived in houses for generations, the decoration and taste of one generation, however inspired, is changed by the next. In big houses, things are consigned to the attic. (I remember in 1988 seeing a bureau inlaid with mother-of-pearl and horn in the style of Boulle, the great French court cabinet-maker of the seventeenth century. Surely no-one who saw it could fail to be bowled over by its exquisite if overwrought beauty. Are you kidding? It lay for a hundred years in an attic at Knole Park whence it was finally hauled down and sold for £1.2 million.) But in smaller houses, things are handed down, sold or get broken and worn out.

I spend a lot of time putting together the rooms where I live. The great master of delightful transient installation in the natural world is the bower bird which constructs elaborate bowers and tunnels adorned with pebbles, feathers, shells, bits of glass, purely for the sake of it or as the dictionary says 'not as nests but as places of resort'. Incidentally, the most beautiful place of resort in England, if you have a passion for houses and ornament, is Sir John Soane's Museum in Lincoln's Inn Fields in London. Here is the classical bower of a great connoisseur. The result of the intellectual powers he turned on building a setting and placing his possessions is both idiosyncratic and sweet decorum. Though room after room is crowded with antiquities and curiosities, there is no feeling of clutter or jumble. I revere John Soane for his major achievement in what is considered, to my mind, wrongly, a minor art; and for the intuitive and exacting discipline he brought to bear on his mania for collecting.

I thought of John Soane and his house as I walked along the Boulevard Malesherbes towards the Camondo Museum, which started life as the house of someone with a dream. For all its beauty, its exquisite quality, over it hangs an unshakeable nightmare. To go from room to room is to walk through accumulation at its most exquisite. You feel that, even when the owner was living there, it was always for show; not to show off but to show or assuage one man's nostalgic passion for what he never had, his efforts to redeem his own racial past and, of course, his consuming passion for the artifacts of a gilded age that still gleams down the centuries. Moise Salomon, Count de Camondo, had a passion for the furniture and decoration of the eighteenth century, a period which for many is the acme of civilised living. He had enough money to buy everything he looked at, but he chose with discrimination.

I remember visiting the gargantuan palaces the American barons built in Newport, Rhode Island, at the turn of the century. They called them cottages – pretension itself – since they were ornate palaces, ostentatious, soul-less advertisements of greed. The Camondo Museum is the opposite; *luxe* to a degree, a confection crammed with beautiful and desirable objects and, though there is nothing quirky there (and my taste runs to oddities), everything is chosen with such passion and care that it is tight as a drum with resonance. The museum, always nearly empty, is a monument to taste, the power of his money and his passion for collecting, but it is not what he meant it to be – a monument to the period it celebrates. Only the very greatest art rises above the guy ropes of its own time; its very construction reveals when it was made. (Tolstoy can do it. When Natasha says to Rostov – 'No, but listen, you're a grown-up man now, aren't you? I'm so glad you're my brother. I want to know what men are really like. Are they like us? Yes? No?' – we're talking magazine cover lines as much as art, as much 1996 as 1812 or 1863.) In general, the time when a thing is painted or written rides roughshod over every attempt to recreate the spirit of another age. A movie made in the 1930s about the Elizabethan period tells us a great deal about the 1930s but not much about the Tudors, and Colin Firth's thighs were never Regency. The spirit of an age cannot be recreated. And so, in many ways, this house, created at the turn of the century, tells us more about the marvellous vanished world of Proust than that of Marie Antoinette.

The great mistake many designers or re-creators make is to show that those who live in a certain age only have the furniture of their time. When you go to a movie or play set in the fifties and see only spindly modern furniture, Bernard Buffet drawings and yellow mugs with hatched lines, you know the set designer has lost the head. Most houses are a jumble of furniture of different periods. That is why the Camondo has an air of unreality and is one of the reasons it makes some people uncomfortable. It is a contrivance, a backdrop for the acting out of a dream life, some other life, which must seem more gratifying or estimable than the creator's given life. But then, that is what all creative work is about. Making a set against which to compose their disordered inner lives is the classic behaviour of the outsider and the artist. People who channel their energies into making their houses beautiful or into collecting never employ an interior decorator and rarely rely on anyone else. Environments like these have nothing to do with a decision, a consideration; for such people to use a decorator would be like asking that person to live their life. Yet, that is what the people who create perfect interiors for the drama – or lack of it – of their own lives, are doing: living another version of their lives that is a world away from the one they led, or might have led, and which would have been literally unbearable. That, too, is why Sir John Soane's Museum seems a living house and not a museum. Here, an extraordinary man lived a passionate existence full of curiosity, and every felicitous object was acquired in a quest for knowledge. Their accumulation seems almost by the way, whereas, in the Camondo, accumulation is the point; each object was acquired, at great cost, because it existed as a supreme example. Its peerlessness is its point. In one sense, this way of collecting is a celebration; in another, a dead-end. Moise de Camondo had a passion for the eighteenth century because of *how* it had been, John Soane for *why* it had been. I belong in spirit to the former category and wish I belonged to the other. And so when I carry, as I always do, a pencil and sketch book to these museums and houses, I draw how pictures were hung, how curtains were used, am agog at the detail of *passementerie*, whereas

I think John Soane would have looked at the boulle and the ormolu and wondered at technique and construction.

The Camondo is implacable in that it never gives an inch in its exquisiteness, its rigorous exclusion of anything that did not meet Moise de Camondo's standards, his determination to spend his existence in a dream of an eighteenth-century golden age. A Jew from Turkey, a man of the highest sensibility, he composed an ideal world, a protection from rebuff and ugliness and malignity. Yet it never does to tempt fate too much in matters of sensibility, and dreams teeter on the edge of horror. Have you heard of the Princess de Lamballe? She had so delicate a nature that she fainted at the sight of a lobster (I'm with her there.) She died in the French Terror with her hacked-off breasts stuffed between her legs to teach her a lesson not to be so nice. Fate can be a bitch. And in a sense the backdrop that Moise de Camondo created in order to lead the life of his dreams (among surroundings that Marie Antoinette would have been utterly familiar with but would not have recognised), became a backdrop for tragedies greater than any dramatist could devise.

It is easy to miss knowing what happened because the legend is so unobtrusive. It is written on a little marble plaque just inside the porch; Moise's beloved son Nissim was killed fighting for France; his daughter and her children were delivered into Auschwitz and died there. This knowledge stirs under the beauty of the house like some feral beast snouting to get out. It makes it uniquely disturbing. The atmosphere is beyond consolation. It also makes me go back and back to walk that mile to celebrate what its creator did, to tell him it's true, that he lived, that he is remembered and that he was a true artist. That great master of decoration, Ingres said, 'Everything has been done, everything has been discovered. Our task is not invention, it is continuity.' It is no task to me but a real labour of love.

WHY ARE THERE NO GREAT
WOMEN ARTISTS?

She said, 'I've got this essay to write in a hurry – why are there no great women artists? Do you know why, Mum?'

Now we have to be careful here, no use rolling on the carpet, spitting tacks and biting dust and getting pointy teeth because the indoctrination is continuous, no use ycelpting names and screaming blue murder about how we wuz robbed, or about how the fact that women do not separate life and art is not recognised as valid. I did all of this anyway while she watched and listened, unmoved, having seen it all before. She then said, 'I have to do it quickly so will you help me?'

'When do you need it for?' I asked.

'Tomorrow,' she replied.

'They can't expect you to do an essay like this in that time,' I said. 'This needs thought and research and talking through.'

'No, it just needs remembering, Mum,' she said. 'You're always going on about it, I just can't remember it all. Anyway, they gave me the title a while ago.'

'How long ago?' I asked.

'Last term,' she said, all innocence. 'So will you help me or not?'

'No,' I said, 'go and remember.' And I called after her, 'Examine who asked the question and why it was asked.'

She came back later. 'It's an aggressive question,' she said. 'My tutor told me that a bloke called Wittgenstein said that a question which was not a true question could not be asked and this isn't a true question. It's not a question at all.'

'It's asked all the time, though,' I said.

'Yes,' she said, 'but it's a well-hostile statement; and its aggression lies in its pretending to be fact. There are great women artists and their work is there to be seen. So the question really should be, *Why* is it not recognised?'

'That's my girl,' I said fondly. I were fair blushing with pride. 'So what's the answer?' I asked.

'I dunno,' she said.

'Go you to your tutor,' I said, 'and tell her you need more time, then get down to this essay; it's important.'

Now I was at the time starting to read a fun book called *Death and the Enlightenment* by John McManners and to postpone the start, was reading his 'Acknowledgements', always a pertinent exercise. And just before that I had received a letter from a friend who was trying to get in her research and her writing while running her household, supporting her poorly husband and looking after her children. The people for whom she was writing made no allowances for her frenzied circumstances. It was her bed, the female bed, and she must lie on it. The 'Acknowledgements' in the Death Book by Professor McManners included thanks to the British Academy for research grants; to a French Foundation for providing the hospitality of Hôtel Chalon-Luxembourg so agreeably situated in the Marais in Paris; thanks to the Rockefeller foundation for a month of agreeable retreat at Bellagio in palatial surroundings by Lake Como; thanks to various scholars for hours of lovely – sorry, read lively there – discourse in flats and restaurants in Paris and in Oxford, in Senior Common rooms, at lunch in Christchurch; thanks to the astonishing forbearance of a woman scholar and her staff who apparently laboured for four years transforming his drafts into typescripts and, in the process of interpreting his handwriting, acquired skills worthy of professional code-breakers and palaeographers; thanks to people who haunted him to hand over incomplete manuscripts; to librarians who devoted their weekends to reading same; to another woman who performed astonishing feats of copy editing on unsystematic references; thanks to his editor, another woman – the most patient and encouraging of people – and, of course, thanks to his wife who relieved him of the burden of compiling an index. I quote, you understand. As I sat reading the long catalogue of complacent selfishness, the pampered existence of your scholarly male writer – and he is not untypical – I could quote others, who never leave home but have trays left outside their doors by their wives, whose telephone calls are intercepted, whose every need is answered, their energies conserved in order to create artistic rubbish – I thought of how any woman struggling to meet the demands made on her would surely be filled, if not with rage, then with envy; but I also reflected that no woman born would be at the receiving end of such babying care or accept it with such orotund complacency. And while I was thus reading of these differing circumstances in the lives of two writers I had encountered, in one morning, via the written word, my daughter was searching for the answer posed by her tutor as to why there are no great women artists.

I might have told her that the answer lies in the search: who is looking, who is defining and who is making the rules; and that many women who should be called artists are declassified by sexist definitions. They have another sort of vision unacknowledged and unsung. But she was writing the essay.

She came back a week later. She said, 'Will you listen for once, really listen? I've worked out that the question or statement is not only aggressive and pretends to be simple but is also a paradox. Women respond to it in a way which almost answers the *why* of it. And the reason they respond like that–' ("Like what?" I asked. "Just *listen*," she said) '–to the *why* of it is because women know deeply, through the way they lead their lives, the difficulties of becoming an artist, in the sense that to *become* it, to be recognised by a lot of work over a lot of years, needs time, commitment and a kind of luxury or maybe selfishness that have traditionally been given to the masculine way of life supported by a woman.'

'Quite so,' I said, 'some day, remind me to show you a certain set of acknowledgements I've just been reading.'

'Don't interrupt,' she said. 'One of the most interesting things about this question, with its hostility built into it, is that men seem to want you to answer it by naming women whose genius and work match people like Rembrandt, say or Michelangelo, who are rare in the whole human race. They should really ask why are there not more artists like Rembrandt or Michelangelo; when you think of how many advantages men have, there should be more. Or else they shouldn't be taken as typical examples.'

'Quite so,' I said.

'Have you heard of someone called Mary Cassatt?' she asked.

'I have,' I said, 'but remind me.'

'An American painter; Degas thought she was one of the greatest painters of his time, although she was almost unknown throughout her life. But it says the advice she gave to American collectors was so perceptive that many of the greatest Impressionist masterpieces went to the US. She said that a woman artist must be capable of making the primary sacrifices. And she did, Mum. She lived alone in Paris, not that I think that's any great sacrifice, and she got on with her work; but do men feel they have to make primary sacrifices in order to do their work? Have you heard of Elizabeth Vigée-Le Brun?'

'Yes,' I said, 'but remind me.'

'Her paintings are brilliant; museums now would like to have her work at any price; but when she was alive she could not get even one institution to show her work. When Sir Joshua Reynolds saw two paintings by her in London, someone asked him what he thought of them and he said they were very fine, as fine as those by any painter living or dead, as fine as Van Dyck and finer. But for centuries people did not even recognise her name, never mind her achievements. Have you heard of John Ruskin?'

'Yes,' I said, 'but remind me.'

'God, he was a male CP, wasn't he? I wrote down some of his sayings: "The masculine intellect is for invention and speculation. But the woman's intellect is not for invention or creation but sweet ordering, arrangement and decision. Her great function is praise."'

'Well,' I said cheerily, 'it's an opinion still held by many priests and politicians and we must battle against this sort of history; while men have been encouraged throughout time to expand their minds, to become great artists, women have had their roles planted elsewhere by men, generally looking after them and their interests.'

'It's true,' she said, 'it's true; do you know Barbara Hepworth? She said that she rarely drew what she saw, but what she *felt* in her body.'

'I'd buy into that,' I said, 'and into that a woman's full awareness of herself as an entity, including her sensations and emotions, informs her work and makes it what it is in its difference and entirety.'

'I can't use that,' she said, 'the tutors would say that we're using gestation metaphors and female biology to make a statement about art; or to make excuses.'

'Oh great,' I said, 'we're kicked right out of the playing field before we even begin simply by being ourselves; we have to deny our femininity in order to be taken seriously.'

'If you go on like that, you'll never be taken seriously,' she said. 'Do you know Frida Kahlo?'

'I know who you mean,' I said, 'and Madonna just bought a painting by her for a million pounds.'

'Yes, and she was married to big fat Diego Rivera who was so keen on attention and praise that he almost gobbled her up and no-one hardly looked at her work when they were alive; and now they think she's great. What I've found is that, when you find the women artists, you see they are great but also that they've had to be these amazing, exceptional women in themselves to be able to leap all the obstacles, mostly erected by men. You know that painting by Vanessa Bell you love? Well, her instructor, he was called Tonks, was lecturing on how a certain painting in an exhibition could not have been done by a woman; no female had the vision or technique to pull it off, then someone pointed out that it was wrongly labelled and had been painted by her. He wasn't ashamed or even embarrassed; he said she might have copied it.'

'It's my turn,' I said. 'Do you know what her sister Virginia Woolf said about a room of your own?'

'I do,' she said, 'our other tutor got us to read that. But there's always odds against us. Do you like Georgia O'Keeffe?'

'I do,' I said.

'Early on, she realised that, if she was to become what she knew she must become, she had to change her life. She wrote "I can't live where I want to, I can't go where I want to, I can't do what I want to – that was nobody's business but my own." So she took off on her own, on her own quest; that's what women should do.'

'But it's a luxury,' I said, 'to be able to be solitary, to not have to deal with anybody else's business. Women have to deal with other people's business – most women, even if they have a room of their own, the door has to be open so they can hear what is going on – they need to; their family depends on that attention but it makes for a split vision, a divided concentration and less time; and time is needed to produce art. You wouldn't have liked it if I had kept my door closed to write while you were a baby. I wouldn't have liked it either.'

'Don't lay any guilt trips on me,' she said. 'Anyway it was often closed. Now are you going to help me write this essay about Elizabeth Vigée-Le Brun, Artemisia Gentileschi, Angelica Kauffman, Mary Delaney, Mary Moser, Meryl Oppenheim, Winifred Nicholson, Laura Knight, Rosalba Carriera, Berthe Morisot, Clara Peeters, Nina Hamnett, Dora Carrington, Sonia Delaunay, Gwen John, Romaine Brookes, Frida Kahlo, Eileen Agar, Helen Chadwick, Helen Frankenthaler, Sarah Purser, Paula Modershon-Becker, Louise Bourgeois, Käthe Kollwitz, Eva Hesse ... or not?'

'Not,' I said.

MIGHTY CRACK

I am sitting at the top of the incline, looking through the frame of the trees towards the house. It's about half a mile away at the spot where I draw it, and makes a perfect miniature, with the look of a doll's house because of its symmetry and simplicity.

When friends go for a walk, arrive at this secret vantage point and notice the house in the distance, they nearly always say one of two things: 'It looks like a doll's house,' says Jack, or 'It looks like a child's drawing,' says Jill.

I think though it would be a sophisticated child who could conceive of the detail. The broad concept is easy enough, with its roof sitting so high, its short, sharply angled planes and brown terracotta tiles, so small an area in proportion to the amount of masonry beneath. And I also think any child drawing such a sliver of roof on such an expanse of house would surely be corrected by a teacher, if corrections happen nowadays or if the teacher does not fear to suppress creativity by a reproof.

Our own Miss MacKeown would never have used the word 'creativity', save in the meaning of 'Genesis' and 'The Creation', and would have been deeply suspicious of the concept; there was no time or space for much creative individual expression in one small classroom with forty children, ranging from eight to fourteen years, who she had to educate without help. And educate she did. Our visual aids were two pictures of the linen industry of North Ireland; a big cracked map of *h-Éireann* with the words '*An Fairrge Mór*' and '*Muir Meann*' writ large all around it; an incomprehensible notice about something called 'Secular', which I thought was one of the Commandments; and an old blackboard perched on its easel on pegs that either worked their way out or were judiciously pushed out by one of the Big Girls seeking diversion.

I might have been anxious about the sins of the Secular, but I was more anxious about the blackboard because I was a Goody-Two-Shoes who always sat in the front row hoping to appease, and knew every teeter of that dangerous edifice. It seemed to me only a matter of time before I was killed. Killing of one kind or another was always on the agenda. Death was threatened for everything: slaughter and mayhem and strangling for a misspelling, homework not done, whispering in class. When the blackboard did one day crash forwards into the crowded classroom, it hit Rosemary, who was also always in the front row, but for opposite reasons – she had been found in a dalliance with the milkman behind the school wall and now Had To Be Watched. When the blackboard fell on her head, her instinctive reaction was not to be stunned, but to kick the shit out of it, while voicing a few ripe oaths which gave a certain amount of insight into the conduct within her own dear family.

I start to draw the house. It is satisfyingly simple, three storeys high, each with three rows of three windows, heavy stone surrounds, nine casements, in fact; so that, although the house was built in the eighteenth century, the windows look a century older. When I first came here, I hated them. I love the wide, clean, glittering, vigorous, classical, above all, grand, panes of glass in big Georgian windows. These small panes, set in their stone surrounds, with their old iron clasps and handles, are not to my taste. When you open them to lean out, you have to angle yourself to get your head and shoulders out, all the while holding onto the clasp so the window won't crash back against the outside wall.

My previous house had grand Georgian windows, and I had never felt the need to open them even on the hottest days; high ceilings kept the rooms cool, and the landscape outside was verified and soothed by the view through such windows, each segment in its fine rectangle tamed into civilised beauty.

But the windows in this house, these I keep open as much as I can. Not just because the views are wild with rampant hedgerows and oaks but because, when they are opened, the sound of the countryside comes rampaging through; horses, sheep, kittens, chickens, rooster, vixens of the prowl, the ratchet noise of pheasants, dying mice squeaking in the jaws of cats, cows calling, and the luring noise of wood pigeon and, in the evening, a nightingale prodigal with its song, and no bloody tractors, no engines at all.

I've made a crack in the noise of our times, I live with the noises of the past, Wordsworth's walnut falling, I'm sick and tired of machine-made noise and I can banish it here. And do.

I begin to draw the chimneys perched at each end, exactly, yes, exactly like a doll's house or a child's drawing, and the path up the middle of the little green lawn in front, and the big trees perfectly in line as though nature too were obeying some dictate of a child's eye and the need for order. I draw in the two small stone plaques high above the main windows. They are carved with letters and numerals and, though far too far away to see, I know the commemorative monograms within them and lean over my work with my finest brush and my magnifying glass. TFD MDCCXXIII I write in one and, in the other, PGA MCMLXXXII. These monograms and Roman numerals were carved nearly three hundred years ago in the shield on the left of the house by its anonymous owners, those on the right by us, the present owners, who will no doubt be equally anonymous in a few years' time.

The men who rebuilt this house for us in 1982 had one thing in common besides their habit of letting their jeans slip inch by provocative inch over their milk white buttocks so there was always a bum cleavage gleaming in the line of vision. Not one of them had a full moniker to call his own. The fashion was for friendly abbreviation: Ken, Chris, Phil, Len, Ernie, Roy, Tel, Dick and, of course, friendliest of all, the abbreviated jeans which showed their botties.

The firm they worked for had been in business in the same premises for well over two hundred years, stretching back at least five generations, which, as I am beginning to learn, is the flicker of an eyelid. Brick on brick all those years. But the old firm was about to go out of business, ruined by recession; its ancient building full of plans and elevations and invoices, pertaining to two and a half centuries of vernacular building in Somerset, to be gutted, the documents to turn up in some antique shop on the Pimlico Road as interesting and quaint documents, devoid of any connection with anything except someone's nostalgia for the past, however near at hand. So much was going to disappear with its closure; not just workers who had been with the firm all their lives; its forge would close too and the glaziers' workshop, the stone masons' shed, the wood carvers' and lintel-makers' long chapel, the builders' yard with its quirky magma – all would close and with them the traditions, apprenticeships and the hard-won shared knowledge of how implacable, beautiful materials are worked and subdued; to be replaced by a huge firm operating out of a brown corrugated cheese of a building on a bypass near a motorway, where a building is a unit, designed by computer and constructed by rote, the window frames stamped out of plastic.

I paint in another row of tiles on the roof and set to work on the unlikely-looking straggling coping, made of sandstone slabs, which hold the tiles in place and give a slightly raffish look to the otherwise primly romantic affair. I start my favourite bit, mixing the brown-red colour of the slabs which fit so precisely into the stone quoins along the edges of the house, the quoins like clamps holding the whole thing erect. Or so you might think.

As I draw, trying to copy, exactly, every detail trim and finite, I think that, if a child had drawn the house as it appears, perched so high on the ground that it looks as though there is a millimetre of space beneath it, a teacher, again, might have pointed out that the lines of a house disappear into the earth, depending on its foundations as a tree needs roots.

But no overseer had corrected that early builder. He had built a three-storey house, with mullioned windows and heavy outcroppings, without bothering about foundations. So the house sits there within its smiling, perfect facade, perched on its slopes, gently sliding forwards inch by inch. And, as I know to my cost, it does not slide all of a piece when it takes its stealthy exercise. Every morning I awake, dreading to see another crack in the wall or ceiling has widened. Five years ago, the engineers and builders took down the back wall, which they had built only seven years before, that fairly important wall – you know, the wall that holds up the roof? – and, propping up the house with a complex jigsaw of joists and beams, they made excavations, twenty feet under, and anchored the house into new foundations fit for Chartres. But that old, early, derelict house had watched the new, abbreviated builders and their slippy, revealing habits closely and decided to do the same and show its pretty cleavage. The expensively and deeply anchored back wall now remains in place; the front and side walls move forwards coyly. Someone gave me a tip. Paste a cigarette paper over the crack. Leave it. Wait. If the paper breaks, then the house has moved. All over the house now are little bits of chasmed paper, pasted onto walls painted by craftsmen who can paint a line around a wall in one stroke, keep it going for many exquisitely straight feet without raising their brush and without dipping once; it takes them years to learn their craft and the only others who can rival them are the men who paint the lines on Rolls Royces. Now there are cracks in these lines where the walls have daintily parted.

So now I sit at the top of the incline looking through the frame of the trees towards the house. It's about half a mile away at the spot where I draw it and makes a perfect miniature, with the look of a doll's house because of its symmetry and simplicity. As I paint, I add in a third little plaque above the door and pencil in a new legend. It is as yet an imaginary plaque, but just as soon as I can lure the stone mason up his ladder, it will be there for all the world to see and learn when it happened. On it will be chiselled in fine roman lettering: *ALIQUIA FISSA AEDIFICIUM DEMONSTRAT, MXM* ('This building showed its cracks, 1996').

HOME THOUGHTS FROM ABROAD

....

How could we have sunk back into the vernacular so quickly? It's the south of France and the skyline stretches towards forever; it's hot, foreign Provence, sunflowers, terracotta, the smell of crushed lavender, brown skin and well being.

Suzanne, whose house this is, comes round the corner to where we are sitting drinking wine on the terrace and says, 'Yous is on the step.' No-one else there could have any idea why we both were so suddenly transported not just into peals of laughter but into another landscape, a place where people fell into sheughs and hoked in the back of presses and dressers and caught themselves on and behaved like ganches, a place where boils and carbuncles of all sorts beeled (and beeling was a Good Thing – it meant the poison was drawing up; I remember the exquisite pain of the hot poultice of milk and bread applied to our beels), a place where people juked in and around corners and had quare consates of themselves, and threw their caps at the cabinet, where you redd up the house before visitors came and the sink where you washed the ware was called the jar box. This shared shorthand of a place is one of the pleasures and rewards of coming from a small place which has held, in some measure, onto its dialect.

Of course, all families have the same private language, words stained by place and associations, a shorthand where you have only to say one word and the family seethes or collapses. All families have many such phrases; my younger sister once was walking down O'Connell Street when she saw ahead of her a smartly dressed woman with the back of her skirt tucked into the back of her knickers the way you can do so easy ... Now Claire has a sensitivity that is almost too finely tuned to ramifications and consequences so she was in a turmoil about whether or not to tell the woman; would she welcome the knowledge or shoot the messenger? She decided that in such circumstances she would much prefer to be told herself, so she overtook the woman and told her as gently and tactfully as possible in such circumstances that she was walking through Dublin with her Janet Regers exposed, although she didn't put it like that. The woman looked at her and said, 'What is it to you?' Ever since, the phrase has only to be muttered within the family for a whole complex of ambiguities to be brought into play, with I'm happy to say, a fair amount of laughter.

Anyway back to the south of France. At dinner that night another guest confessed he lived in dread that a certain woman was going to pursue him from New York; he thought there was a good chance she would suddenly turn up. To tell you the truth, all of us thought he was rather boastful and a bit given to wishful thinking, but lo, while he was out trawling Mazamet for lavender oil and woven baskets and hand-milled soaps and long-haired goats' cheese – yep, we picked the hairs off before we ate it – your woman turned up in a taxi. We all jostled and shoved and composed our faces into earnest expressions of delight and surprise.

'He has a hard time expressing his wishes ... we all do, we Americans,' she said. 'He finds it hard to say to me "I'd so much like you to be there".' We none of us looked at each other. She went out to sit on the white wall the better to surprise him on his return, and we busied ourselves at jobs that somehow needed doing well within eye and earshot of the moment when he would step out of his car with his ethnic treasure trove and no inkling.

Suzanne said to me, 'He's going to get a quare gunk,' and we had to run off and roll in the grass, stuffing clothes into our mouths to stop the gurgling noises. Then he drove up, I saw his face, and I haven't, as they say in Tamnamore, cast the cool of it yet.

At dinner that night, sitting on the terrace with France stretching scented into the azure distance and sounds of angry American voices above our heads, Tom told us of his visit to Egypt; whilst there he'd had a rush of blood to the head and bethought himself to have made a sharp and natty white suit; indeed he was wearing the self-same suit and, being long, thin and blonde, looked wonderful; maddened by his success he decided what was needed to complete the swank was a fez. These turned out to be difficult to find, not being wholly politically correct but at last he found a man who could make one – scarlet with a gold tassel, a hat fit for a pasha or potentate. When he walked out of the little back-street shop wearing suit and fez he found himself being followed by a crowd of children shouting, '*King Farouk! King Farouk!*' Nothing fazed, he considered how many of his friends back in Bristol would love such a feeling as a fez gives so he ordered half a dozen more and brought them home. He and his mates put on their fezzes and went down for a pint to their local Slug and Lettuce. As they came in through the door of the pub, the landlord, without missing a beat, pointed at the door and shouted. 'No fezzes; no fezzes; house rule; no fezzes, out out out!' and they had to leave.

I hadn't planned to go to France at all, since I had just come back from an idyllic holiday in Spain in the same house we've been going to for twenty years and which surpasses description; just before we left, we got a casual postcard from a friend inviting us to the seventieth birthday party of her husband – A Surprise Party, a dinner on Saturday night. These are seriously good party-givers and the big Seven-O is quite a landmark, so I made happy noises until my husband pointed out there was a little local difficulty. The party was to be held in their house in the South of France, behind St Tropez (the house used to belong to Jeanne Moreau and is stunning).

Now I don't have the lifestyle, Latin or equipment to be able to make it to the south of France for a dinner party, and so, reader, when my putative hostess rang, I lied, with genuine regret, that we wouldn't be back from Spain. Well, talk about throwing the bull over the bridge. 'What a pity,' she said. 'I was going to send the jet to pick you up.'

There was a long silence. She is very clever as well as very beautiful. She waited. I waited. Then I said, being so sophisticated and all, 'But, Regine, you couldn't land a jet at Cannwood; it's too hilly.'

There was another silence, this time the stunned one that comes from someone absorbing another's true state of ignorance. 'No, darling,' she said. 'We would send it to Farnborough which is only forty-five minutes from you, you'd land at Nice and we'd have had the helicopter bring you the rest of the way. I'm so sorry you can't come ...'

'So am I,' I said glumly, well hoisted.

I shuffled upstairs to where my husband was writing. 'Guess what I've done,' I said.

He lifted the phone. He said, 'Regine, we'll be at Farnborough just whenever it suits.'

'Fine, darling,' she said. 'I couldn't be more delighted.' Then they both laughed like drains.

I don't suppose I've ever eaten more delicious humble pie than the caviar and champagne we had sitting on board in armchairs watching the clouds stream by, a little border terrier on my lap – a birthday present sent by someone else. It was, I'm happy to report, one of the best birthday parties ever, with a Cuban salsa band and a rock group from Glasgow, plus everything else, and a woman who warned me I must never dive because diving shatters emeralds. I could get used to life like that. Then I went on to visit my friend Suzanne in her house in another part of the south of France. When she came round the corner and said, 'Yous is on the step', I knew I was back at home in Ulster.

A few hours later I got a telephone call from another part of home, from Dublin, a friend calling to say old Mrs Tabiteau, my next-door neighbour had died and with her one of the last vestiges of the old, proud, professional, Protestant Dublin folk descended from Huguenots.

To say Mrs T liked cats is like saying children like Christmas; at one count we reckoned she had thirty cats living in and about her small house and garden. She was a beautiful, white-haired woman, but tiny, and in her car could hardly be seen over the top of the steering wheel by anyone outside the vehicle, and when Yum-Yum was run over in front of her house, she drove like the clappers to the Charlemont veterinary hospital so that, although Yum-Yum lost one of her eyes, her life was saved. I often wonder what Dublin commuters made of a Morris Minor hurtling at high speed across red traffic lights, apparently without a driver, but with a mad-eyed, tear-drenched woman in the passenger seat. I can write about this event now, but at the time it nearly broke my heart.

This is how it happened: I set out across the street with my little dogs to go to the park. They were on long, retractable leads. To this day, I don't know how it happened or why. All I remember is a deep and dreadful thud, a high, chilling scream of pain and the sound of a car speeding on. Two girls, driving a jeep, going in the other direction, saw me kneeling with Yum-Yum in the street and with great kindness helped me back to my house and stayed with the other dogs while Mrs Tabiteau got us to the Charlemont where Mr Hardy the vet was waiting. As she drove, head down, dander up, and I tried to hold my little dog's eyes in place, my mind was filled with images of Yum-Yum as she had been, with her endearing, squashed-up face, lustrous globular eyes, her little fountain of a tail curling over a back arched like a bridge, and then what I saw after the car hit her, eyes pouring down her face, tail in the dust, body bent the other way, the bridge terribly foundered and the noise, coming not out of her mouth, but out of her body, which I held while it got cooler and stiller. I cursed (and still curse) the driver who was going at such a speed that in his haste he couldn't even stop for me or a dog.

After Mrs Tabiteau's death I inherited her two pugs, Archie and Jamie, which means that, one way or another, I now have six small dogs. Both Archie and Jamie were subdued and quiet when I first got them – and who wouldn't be, losing the person who loved them, going to a new owner, a new house and four, terrible, hostile, watchful, resident beasts to boot; not only that, but Jamie had run from Mrs Tabiteau's house soon after she died and was found in Clonskeagh. How he crossed some of the roads in Dublin without being killed, I'll never know, nor will the angelic family who rescued him, and that adventure had shaken him up.

All the same they have, as you might say, settled in almost to a fault, and Archie beats all. Soon after he arrived, his eyes fell out – (what is it with me and dogs' eyes?) and for a while after the vet had stitched them back in, Archie was made to wear a plastic thing around his neck which, although it made him look like a small, fat, fawn thing stuck in a colander or a small, fat, fawn thing wearing a lampshade, somehow didn't stop him sinking teeth in legs and hanging onto trousers and Wellington boots, preferably inhabited. The postmen threatened to stop delivering, the plumber turned and left, the greenhouse builders are still aloft. But I love him more than life itself as I do all my dogs and no matter that if you put them all together, you might, with luck get one entire dog, I still think they are beautiful.

One last little dog story, then I promise I'll never tell another. Last week, a couple came down the lane in a car with a beautiful little collie without a collar crouched in the back. It was very sad and cringey, they had found it wandering along a road miles from anywhere and as they were going away the next day asked if I would look after it till its owner could be found.

I hated it being so sad and frightened and remembered one of the things that most distressed me when I lost Loulou was the knowledge that she might never hear her own name again. So I said to my husband – who as you will gather is bored patience itself – 'I wish at least we knew its name.'

'Call her Lassie,' he said, 'she looks like Lassie.'

'Talk about showing your age,' I said. 'I'll call her Bessie.' At which the dog stopped looking quite so woebegone and stepped across the room, waving her tail a little tentatively.

'Bessie?' I said, 'Bessie?' She positively glowed. So Bessie she became. We put out all the calls to the vets, the rescue centres, the police and eventually a woman rang, with that tremor in the voice I know so well, and said, 'Have you got a little black and white collie?'

'I have,' I said. She burst into tears.

'She's a sweet dog,' I said, 'and I christened her Bessie. What's her real name?'

'That's her real name,' she said, so we both had a sniffle.

When I related the story to Suzanne in the south of France

to show my spiritual link with the animals, she said, 'You're a tarra,' and all our friends watched as two grown women laughed till they cried.

THE ARK

I'm sounding more and more like the Ancient Mariner and you are the hapless Wedding Guest and till my ghastly tale is told, This heart within me burns ... My story is this: Sometimes you see a letter in the newspaper or read a report that leaves you reeling because of its touching ignorance of present-day conditions; they are written by other-planet people or holy fools. It is harder to take when the airheads are Our Leaders. When he was Prime Minister, John Major delivered a superb specimen to the Conservative Group for Europe which, if spoken by anyone else, might have been thought a whimsical parody (if only), 'Long shadows on country grounds, warm beer, invincible green suburbs, old maids bicycling to Holy Communion through the morning mist ...' Hello? Old maids bicycling to Holy Communion through the morning mist? I think that even beats my number one slot, hitherto occupied by de Valera's speech about comely maidens and dancing at the crossroads. I've just read another one, a letter in the *Irish Times*, from a man who now lives in Ballsbridge in Dublin. He wrote that he grew up in England fifty years ago, where everywhere he saw buttercups and daisies. In 1947 he went to South Africa, where again there were plenty. Now he has come to live in Ireland, and he asks what has happened to Irish buttercups. 'Has some strange disease hit them?' Well, yes. The twentieth century has hit them, then they were jumped on while they were down, by those mercenaries of our times – farmers. How could he not *know*?

Increasingly I find I'm surrounded by people living in cloud-cuckoo land, who somehow manage to protect themselves from what is happening all around them; either that or they are dunces. Just look at events of the past few years. A ship is speared on top of a spike and seventy-five thousand tons of crude oil pour out into the sea. Blame the British government, blame the pilot, blame the weather, but don't blame the proprietors of these floating hulks with no double-skinned hulls and no contingency back-up – so if the huge tin box is punctured, the whole lot comes pouring out. Dolphins, molluscs, birds, fish – all doomed to a foul death. Each spillage gets horrified publicity as if it was a once-off when, in fact, ships regularly clean out their bilges at sea and the continuous damage to marine life is incalculable. Not perhaps as terrible as the over-fishing that goes on all the time, and less terrible than what many observers believe to be true – that the waters around our islands are more radically polluted by Sellafield accidents than by any oil spillage.

We live in an ark that is sinking. Every year the world loses thousands of species; gone for ever. Some biologists think we may be losing one species per day. The problem is worst in the tropics where human populations are increasing (although if these countries start using plastic the way Western civilisations do, they're not going to keep that up. The sperm count of young males is down by twenty-five per cent and biologists think it is caused by the increased use of plastics.) In what is called the 'Third World', they face overwhelming economic problems, and conservation is hardly high on their list of priorities. To urge these nations to spend time and money on saving species at risk, must appear to them a form of neo-imperialism or a luxury they cannot afford. One way and another, it is only a matter of time until thousands and thousands of species of plants and animals have disappeared into the galactic cold. When these things die they go for good. Man cannot re-constitute them. They are extinct. For me the word 'extinct' is another word for mass murder. These beasts and birds go into a dark night, from which there is no returning, a dark night into which we will surely follow.

Do you know about canaries? How they were brought down into pits by miners? If the canaries died, the miners knew to get out fast. There are human beings who are canaries; their equivalent is not dying but asthma, allergies and depression. Those who do not sink under illness or depression and become almost inert, trapped by grief and prophecy, become active in trying to redeem anything; some, often risking life and limb, join in active protest, others join organisations like Greenpeace or Friends of the Earth who work to halt our tribal suicide; more and more people are becoming vegetarian in an effort to do something about that other related issue, the cruelty that we inflict ceaselessly on the other inhabitants of the world we share.

You know, I am sure, the analogy; one rivet falls out of the aeroplane, it keeps on flying; ten fall out, it keeps on flying; twenty fall out, it keeps on flying; one more drops out, the plane crashes. We've lost a lot of rivets lately.

Some of you reading this may think you do not contribute to the death of species. We all do. Do you use peat in your garden? There are wonderful peatlands and bogs in Ireland but they are disappearing fast. The Irish Peatland Conservation Council (IPCC) works hard to get the peatlands listed as special areas for conservation. It needs help. The Irish government is lagging behind on its commitment to deliver a list of peatlands to the European Union; soon there will be no time for conservation groups to study and make amendments to the list, then we'll have another of those dismaying, half-arsed compromises that don't work. In the meantime, the IPCC is buying as much bogland as it can; it could do with a little help from you.

We all know about the corncrake; its harsh cracking call, which was so much part of Irish rural life, has all but disappeared. Birdwatch Ireland is trying to save the last remaining corncrakes on the Shannon Callows, North Donegal and Mayo.

The problem is that the corncrake is a migratory bird, so you cannot just re-introduce it; its migratory instincts are set on the area where it was born. If a farmer, greedy for a rood of land, another shilling to his income, mows in such a way, and at such a time, that its legs are chopped off as it stays with its young, faithful to the end, then that is the price the farmer is prepared to pay. Never mind we're paying *him*. And you can't induce a captured corncrake to go where it's safe. It doesn't know *how*, it has to answer the imperative of its migratory urge.

We can all try to help. Those plastic bags you pick up in every shop are lethal. All plastic is. Sea turtles, entangled in curtains of plastic fishnet, die slowly. Seal and sea pigs, snouts clamped shut by plastic rings from a six-pack, suffocate slowly; herring gulls starve to death, necks encircled by such rings. Sea lions become entangled in plastic line and die, trying desperately to wriggle free. Many sea animals die because of ingesting plastic gloves. On land, countless small mammals die in glass bottles and beer cans; once in, they cannot climb back up the smooth sides. Twenty-nine little corpses were found in one glass bottle in an English wood.

I believe, gloomily, that there is a more radical stopper to all our efforts to save wildlife. Living things lose heart. Literally. In one sense, when the heart of their community goes; in another, when the odds are too long and they give up. This I think is what is happening to us. The heart of a community is not an easy thing to pinpoint. I'll give you two examples: one is the story of the passenger pigeon, a native of North America – from Canada to the Gulf of Mexico. There were billions, the male, slate blue, with a russet breast and white abdomen. The young were fed on milk produced by both male and female. At the beginning of the nineteenth century, when they were migrating, the days were darkened; sometimes, as the birds arrived for nesting, the sky was black for mile upon mile. People spoke of flocks a hundred miles wide. To the settlers in America, the birds were an invaluable source of food. They were hunted by bands of professional shooters, used as bait in trap shooting. Even in the 1880s after relentless butchery, they still numbered millions. Then, quite suddenly, they died. They needed those enormous flocks to create the conditions for continued life. The last passenger pigeon, a bird called Martha, died in Cincinnati Zoo in 1914.

The second, more recent, story is happening now. Many amphibians and reptiles are simply sliding off the scale. Frogs are disappearing. In the US, where research is advanced, biologists have found that ponds which once echoed thunderously to sounds of bullfrogs are now silent. Millions of toads have always hatched in a place called Lost Lake where, in all the years it has been monitored, there was never more than five per cent mortality. Then in 1990, fifty per cent of two milllion eggs did not hatch. Last year only a few thousand hatched. In Australia, biologists have not seen a certain species – the gastric brooding frog – which raises its young in its stomach (remind you of anyone?) since 1980. Frogs are vanishing from Denmark, Nova Scotia, Peru, Panama, Switzerland, the UK, India. Amphibians, among the oldest creatures on earth, evolved more than 350 million years ago. If they are dying off, we're in serious trouble. They really are the canaries of our environment, with dual habitats, so they get the worst of both worlds – contaminated earth and polluted water. Their skin is as vulnerable to ultraviolet rays as ours – or more so. And everything is so connected to everything else. Before the war, white storks sat on the roofs of many German towns. They don't any more. They fed mainly on frogs.

Every day comes a report of another rivet dropping out. Recently, the mouse-eared bat became extinct in England. Many other species of bat are on the verge of extinction. An integral part of our ecology, neither pests nor rodents, they are necessary for the cycle which eventually keeps us alive. They eat only insects, but, because of increased use of pesticides by farmers and the loss of rich meadows, and marsh and peatlands, they have lost their food source. You, reading this, who want the cheapest food and make no protest about farming methods, are contributing to your own decline. Biologists say they do not know what is happening – they're a conservative bunch and need a lot of time and data to talk definitively. Well, they don't have time, and I can tell them why. Look to the passenger pigeon. In fact, I'm amazed more species don't just give up. Fish in rivers and oceans must live in terror. As all living creatures do, they communicate with each other, and the tom-toms signalling danger between their shoals must tell them that everywhere they turn lies destruction. I'm sure falling stocks are not just to do with over-fishing. It has to do with losing heart, being frightened to death.

Two hundred years ago, Blake wrote:

> A dog starv'd at his master's gate
> Predicts the ruin of the State.
> A horse misus'd upon the road
> Calls to heaven for human blood

Each outcry of the hunted hare.
A fibre from the brain does tear
A skylark wounded in the wing
A cherubim does cease to sing.

What is odd is that political parties do not appear to take note of these concerns shared by so many people. In this country we are guilty of not taking enough heed of expensive research carried out in other countries. Take the badger. Anyone who knows badgers can hardly bear to think of how this nocturnal mammal is persecuted. Never mind how it is run down in its thousands by gurriers who drive through country roads at sixty miles an hour. Never mind how in Wales it is trapped, its legs or back broken, and sent to Ireland for dog fights. Over 150 years ago John Clare wrote about the barbaric sport in stinging terms:

Though scarcely half as big, demure and small
he fights with dogs for hours and beats them all.
Till kicked and torn and beaten out he lies
and leaves his hold and cackles, groans and dies.

This still goes on. Badger baiting is on the increase in Ireland, and there is no proper organisation amongst the *gardaí* to deal with it. In England, badger baiting is treated as a crime with jail sentences and heavy fines; as a result more of these perverts travel to Ireland to engage in their horrible practices. They use the word 'sport'; blood sport indeed. It makes me ashamed to be human.

But these are aberrations. What is unforgivable is official endorsement of the killings. For years and years in Gloucestershire where I lived, farmers, backed by the Ministry of Agriculture, ruthlessly tried to exterminate badgers because of the vexed question of transmission of TB to cattle. After twenty years, this policy has not reduced the incidence of disease in cattle. Yet, last year, the *Irish Farmers Journal* had headlines about the badgers' role in the spread of TB; now it appears there is to be another wholesale war against the badger in certain counties in Ireland – funded by the government. It is as if all the killing, all the research in England, was for nothing. Nothing. That black and white, snuffling, ancient thing, paddling away in single file to fossick out insects, will be persecuted in the most vile way, its young left to die in their setts on the basis of unscientific, unproven evidence. Not many cherubim are singing in Offaly.

Since 1989 the numbers of the common sparrow have declined by half; the lapwing has dropped by over seventy per cent in the past fifteen years; skylarks have declined by half over the past twenty years. The decline in the numbers of the sparrow, bullfinch, corn-bunting, coal-tit, tree sparrow, is linked to the decline of seed scattered in the farmlands. In the west of Ireland, the alders are dying; the hazel blackthorn, elderberry and hawthorn do not flower as they used to. The blackthorn has stopped producing sloes in the same quantities; the hazel nut produces dry husks. They are dying and so are we. But the difference is that we are doing the killing, and we are also killing the future. Every extinction foreshadows our own.

A blink ago in the evolutionary scale, the yellow bittern became extinct in Ireland. In another blink it will be us. 'The lark, the corncrake and the grouse/ Will bring good luck to any house' ran an old Borders song. The good luck is going fast unless we have a mind to stop it. You can write to the Minister for Agriculture, asking for proof and assessment on the badger question; you can tell your representative in government how you feel about hare coursing; you can support the many organisations that are trying to halt the decline in our species. Put pressure on farmers to stop their cruel practices. You can stop using plastic bags, be careful about your rubbish, stop using the car so much, pressure the authorities to provide better public transport. You can do all sorts of things, but most of you won't. Well, as Sarah, who looked after me when I was a child and who I loved, used to say when I wouldn't listen: 'Don't be coming running to me afterwards.' There won't be any Sarahs when the future has run out.

After I had finished writing this with a heavy heart, I got a letter from the Royal Society for the Protection of Birds (RSPB) and Birdwatch Ireland. The Irish government had announced a partial commitment to corncrake conservation measures; in 1995/96 there was a fifteen per cent increase in the numbers of corncrake in England, and, in Ireland, an increase of thirty-five per cent was recorded. The numbers are small, but the slide into extinction has been prevented. My heart is singing, never mind the cherubim. And the RSPB are coming to discuss the possibility of our land being managed to help other species. Maybe I feel a flicker of hope. Do you remember the last lines of 'The Ancient Mariner'?

> He prayeth best, who loveth best
> All things both great and small;
> For the dear God who loveth us,
> He made and Loveth all.

BORDER-LINE CASE

You can always tell when you are leaving a Protestant area in Northern Ireland and entering a Catholic one. The roads deteriorate. You are reminded, at every jolt, of old sores, they rattle back up to the surface as the car bumps along. Forty years ago we had a car, EGW 851, with running boards that we clung to like barnacles. For years it was the only one in the parish, save for the parish priest's Mayflower which, with its razor-sharp edges, cut through the parish like something out of *Jaws*, seeking to devour the sinful. My father drove his Austin with panache. He was the son of the local JP, who was an erstwhile agent of de Valera's, his brother was the Doctor, and he himself was an athlete with county records to his name. Such things counted enough then to make him distinctive in our small province. But they counted for very little when we were stopped as we bumped our way home out of Cookstown, down towards the lough shore where our tribe lived. Every time we passed the good land further inshore which had been ours before the Plantation, we looked at it, though without rancour – our rushy pastures had their compensations for children, and my father had never said a bitter word. All the same the rancour came later, a rank need sprouting from seeds sown long ago.

Forty years ago, the security checkpoints were mobile and you never knew where or when they would suddenly appear. They came in vehicles, in force and in uniform – they were the 'B' Specials, an auxiliary police force organised by the UK government in 1920 and taken over by the Northern Ireland government. It was a voluntary police force organised on a county basis, with about ten thousand members, and it was one hundred per cent Protestant and, Catholics believed, one hundred per cent Orange. It was a provocative and dismaying thing for a government to do – to oganise a voluntary, licensed band of armed men from one section of the community, and give them arms and power. We believed they could sniff a Catholic in a car like rats round strange bread. Every time they stopped my father, handsome, distinctive, driving one of the few cars in the district for miles around, they would haul him out of the car and question him as to his business, his identity, his destination. It was meant to be ritual humiliation and it never appeared to work. We kept quiet in the back of the car. We didn't know much but we knew enough to be frightened. After it had happened a number of times, and even as a child I recognised the same men asking him the same questions, I asked, 'But didn't they know you?'

'They knew me like a begging ass, daughter.'

'So why did they stop and ask you who you were like that when they know?'

'To put manners on me,' he said.

No man needed putting manners on less, but it was my first experience of the prejudice and discrimination that floated out from Stormont, shrouding Catholics in discouragement, reducing our chances, stopping representation by gerrymandering and chicanery.

The leader of the ruling caste, Lord Brookeborough, a man of near-absolute power, made no secret of the fact that he despised Catholics. This man, who was for so many years our Prime Minister, and who, through a kind of lazy viciousness, did so much damage to the province, once bestirred himself enough to call publicly on Protestants not to employ Catholics. ('I have *not* one about the place,') though legend has it all the same that his cook was Catholic.

Years later, under pressure from Westminster, the 'B' men were disbanded, barrelled back to their corners and there they waited. They knew their time would come round again.

And indeed it has. The violence that for so many years has bedevilled the province has made a fine smoke-screen for rank anti-libertarian attitudes to flourish. In Northern Ireland, policemen can harass anyone under the coverall of a question of security, when it has nothing to do with security. Everywhere you go there are crowds of policemen in their flak jackets, united in their numbers and strength, waiting to show who's boss. On one day's driving through Northern Ireland a few years ago, I had a series of encounters which would not be countenanced anywhere else in these islands and which encroached on my liberty, and those who encroached were using official cars, were being paid by the tax-payer, were on official duty and behaved like thugs. I relate only one of these incidents here.

It was a fine Saturday in August and I was driving from Belfast to Warrenpoint. I was driving my husband's car, which unlike my own, is an automatic, and I reached the village of Moy, near Armagh, once the fiefdom of James Caulfeild, Lord Charlemont, bibliophile, dandy, soldier, queller of insurrection in Ulster, and the man who built the Casino at The Marino and whose townhouse is now the Hugh Lane Gallery in Parnell Square (Rutland Square in his day). At the entrance to the town I was stopped by two policemen and asked to wait, as a procession was marching through the town. I pulled in, switched off and waited. I don't know what I expected; small, solemn children in white dresses? Some kind of feria? Mummers perhaps, or pageants on floats? Then I remembered: Lady's Day, 15 August, the Feast of the Assumption, is one of the two days the Hibernians march; I looked forward to hearing the old tunes. Then I heard the approaching noise and knew this was a different sound of music. This band and these marchers were something else. There was no gaiety, no laughter. Men dressed in bowler hats, dark suits and orange sashes colonised the day in a sinister fashion, marching as if to war. If one had seen such a group in Albania, say, or in some fastness of Latvia, one would have been fascinated by the folkloric display. But these were the Black men, the elite of the Orange Order. The Orange Order is reckoned to have over a hundred thousand members and is a powerful political and lobbying force. It acts as a focus for bigotry and extremism, and, traditionally, to rise in the Unionist Party it was essential to be an Orangeman. The Orange parades often marched through Catholic areas for the sake of it. Here they were again. My heart sank. Twenty-five years on and I'm listening to the same harsh beat I used to hear every July and August throughout my childhood. The members of these bands practise an aggressive drumming technique, especially exponents of the 'big Slapper', the large diameter lambeg drum, and as they march their faces are rigid, their territory is spoored. It would truly be hard to feel any warmth or pleasure watching the members of an Orange band, their faces hard as the hobs of hell, strutting their stuff as though they owned the place. Which they think they do.

I waited in my car looking ahead. My little dogs flung themselves at the windows. Other cars drew up behind. We all waited. The march passed by, ugly in its triumphalism. I tried to drive off. Behind me, the row of cars revved, but my engine seemed dead. I slightly panicked, swore, tried again and then, remembering I was driving an automatic, put the gear into drive. The car jumped forward as though stung and lurched off; the other cars following. A hundred yards further along the road I saw a police officer step into the road, talking into his mouth mike and pressing his earphones hard. He flagged me down, waved the other cars on. I rolled down the window.

'Pull over to the side,' he shouted. 'Pull over.' I heard him say into his mike, 'I have her here.'

He leaned in through the window of the car and the dogs sprang at him in a frenzy of outrage. They may be the insects of the canine world but they have bottle. He pulled back sharpish. I tried to silence them.

'What's wrong?' I asked, above the barking.

'You're being detained,' he said.

'Detained? Why? What for?'

'For shouting and cursing back there.'

'For *what?*' I couldn't believe my ears.

An unmarked car screeched up and a big policeman jumped out and came running over. I had seen him and his like often before. Forty years before. A 'B' man. Same look, same manners, same – dislocated anger.

'We'll soon see about this,' he said. 'What's wrong with you?'

'There's nothing wrong,' I said.

'Oh aye, there is, miss,' he said, 'cursing and shouting at the marchers back there. I seen you. I seen you. Miss Madam.'

'I never got out of the car,' I said. I was bewildered and I have to say frightened. 'I don't know what you're talking about.'

He ran across the road to another car and back again, manic, his hands frantic.

'You were in yer car,' he said, 'and you were seen to curse and swear. What's your date of birth?'

I was so stunned by this *non sequitur* that I told him. He ran to the back of the car, demented, shouting, banging on the boot and I started to get out of the car. 'Get back,' he shouted. 'Get you back in.' I climbed back in hastily. The two other policemen stood at each side of the car as though it was a mad animal.

'Where's your licence?' he said. 'We'll soon see about this, we'll soon see about this, cursing and shouting at marchers. Where are you from?'

'I live in Somerset,' I said.

'I see that,' he said, snatching the licence. 'I can read. I can read. But what I read is not where you're from. Your name is Devlin, Mrs Devlin, and that's not from Somerset. I know where you're from.' He banged the top of the car again, which set the dogs off like smoke alarms.

'What's this all about?' I said. My voice was weak, placatory. 'What did I do? I haven't *done* anything.' I was so upset that I was nearly in tears.

He turned away, his face black, and ran back to behind the car, and then back across the road to where his colleague was getting data from his car's computer. I thought of my father, the number of times they had stopped him for no good reason just to show him who was boss, and I remembered his mannerliness, his intrinsic courtesy, and I took a deep breath and calmed myself. Across the road the policemen conferred on the radio. They kept looking across at me. The waves of anger were almost palpable. Why? Because someone in the march hadn't liked the way I looked? Because someone hadn't liked my demeanour as I moved off? They were still talking into the radio. Northern Ireland has the best security system in the world. In a matter of milli-seconds they know who owns the car you are driving and where it's from and, for all I know, where you are going.

I don't know if I have conveyed the levels of anger and hostility surrounding me, but all I could do was wait and shiver and stroke the dogs as the big, uniformed men terrorised a single woman in a car for no reason whatsoever, other than she had not smiled and waved as a band representing everything that is hateful to her marched past. The men were still at their car radio or computer or whatever they have in their patrol cars, but now they were looking over at me and conferring ...

Now, I have an OBE (for services to literature, since you ask, and no laughing at the back of the class), an honour presented by the Queen. This, though not on my driving licence, is always used on letters sent to me from the Northern Ireland administration. Perhaps the police computer has this Establishment-friendly information on it, or perhaps the computer told them that I had a connection, however tenuous, with the press. Whatever; something did the trick. From being one of Them, I became one of Us. The big officer came back from his information centre with a different demeanour. 'What's your occupation, Mrs Garnett?'

'I'm a writer,' I said, angry with myself for parleying with him.

'That's some job you have there,' he said. 'Maybe you'll put me in a book sometime.' He looked at me consideringly and banged the top of the car with his hand, but more gently this time. The dogs leapt up like missiles, howling horribly.

'Good wee watchdogs, miss,' he said. 'Go you on now. It was a bit of a mistake. All the best now. All the best.'

Now I know I should have taken his name and number but hindsight is easy after an event. When, shaken, I reached Warrenpoint and told friends of the harassment, the questioning, the threats in the course of an ordinary morning's motoring, they were sympathetic but unsurprised. It happened a lot.

Back in England someone who should have known a great deal better said, when I related the story, 'You lot brought it on yourselves.' Blame the victim because to look at the aggressor involves too thorough an examination of the system in power.

NIGHT JOURNEYS

Among a welter of books and papers on the table beside my bed lies a pencil and paper. I seem to remember Margaret Drabble saying she had at last understood the nature of mortality when she stopped fretting about not having enough time to read all the books in the world she wanted to read, and began to fret about not having the time to finish all the books on her bedside table. I munch through the vast pile like a defeated moth starting in on a huge fur coat, knowing it will never get to the end, yet, for the love of it, unable to give up. The pile is, of course, constantly being added to, so that what were once new books have now gained the status of Modern First Editions (mint condition, I might add). I sometimes think to be a rich woman I only have to sell the contents of the bedside table (oh, all right, less poor).

I keep the pencil and paper to write down my dreams when I remember them. Can you imagine anything more boring? But I was told to by my therapist, and I had obedience beaten into me as a child (what Irish Catholic had not?). I went to him for years, fourteen years regularly – can you imagine how mad I was? And has it helped? I hear you cry, and, yes, yes, I answer. I am more of everything now; more disturbed, more mad, more dreams, more better. Dreams are a key to life, and the theory is that, if you remember them, they have an import – i.e., your unconscious wants the conscious to look at them and learn. The unconscious is an idiot if, after fifty years of living with me, it thinks I'm going to listen to anything I don't want to listen to. I am adept as Ian Paisley at not looking at what I don't want to see. However, I follow the good, dear therapist's instructions (no, *of course*, I mean suggestions) and write down the imaginative adventures of the night. I think that dreaming permits each and every one of us to be quietly and safely insane every night of our lives. Dreams are not prophesies: they don't tell what is going to happen, but they illuminate what *is* happening and in a way that is a step forward into the future. They can also give salutary warnings to slow down.

Imagination is a divine power and enjoying the use of this power brings a strength of personal vision. I see, in the merger of the dreamer and the waking person, some kind of truth; occasionally, I see a dark glimpse of who I was and, as it is not a nice picture, I shove the evidence into a folder labelled 'Recipes' and pretend they never happened, that such things don't lurk in my dreams. Repression is the name of my game. In the game of darts, there is a scam called 'thick chalk', which scorers use to turn a three into an eight, say, to up their score; I find that, when I waken from a vivid dream and write it down, my mind has used thick chalk – everything is larger than life and out of kilter, not adding up to what I know, but something strange, often morbid and fantastical, a world in which I, strangely attired, negotiate with people in a way I could not in real life.

But besides the fantastical and larger than life dreams, the ominous ones, the ones that reveal to me the inner preoccupations that I haven't allowed to surface, there are also what you might call, if you weren't too particular, literary dreams. I often dream about writing and waken fretting about what I have lost, sure that I was missing out on all manner of great things; poems would flash into my head fully grown; great slogans; once even, the perfect quiz game that the BBC would kill for; in the morning all gone, gone utterly. I was cheered in my sense of loss when I chanced to read the story of William Tickle, an eighteenth-century Scottish poet who also endlessly regretted he could not remember the poetry he composed in his sleep, which was, he believed, infinitely superior to anything he produced in his waking hours. One morning, he awoke and yet again began to lament to his long-suffering wife that he had just lost forever the most sublime poetry ever written.

'What!' said his wife, 'were you writing poetry?'

'Yes,' he replied, 'and such poetry that I would give the world to remember it.'

'I heard it,' she said, 'and I remember the last lines exactly. They were:

> By heaven I'll wreak my woes
> Upon the cowslip and the pale primrose.

Robert Browning was a famous dreamer who showed, in his recounting of tales from his unconscious, a sense of humour missing from his poems. 'Once I dreamed I was seeing the elder king in *Richard the Third,* and he uttered a line which struck me as immensely finer than anything else in the play, or anything I had ever heard perhaps, and I perceived it was not Shakespeare's, but my own invention. It was in the scene where ghosts rise. When I woke I still had hold of the stupendous line and it was this:

> And when I wake my dreams are madness –
> damn me!'

Reading this rather cheered me for if a great poet dreams only in banalities, then it is unlikely I was composing timeless sonnets under cover of night. But I placed a pencil and paper by my bedside and determined to record what I could remember of my night-time thought-life and write it all down. So half awake, half asleep – what's the difference? – I scribbled a graffiti record of the mayhem that went on in the corridors of dream. I'd fall back into a deep sleep and, half the time, in the morning, I couldn't even read my scrawl wandering across the pages at odd angles. But sometimes I could and mostly it helped. I found out what was literally preoccupying me. It's a wonderful word that, if you analyse it – your interior occupied by stuff you haven't worked out or jettisoned.

Then last night, i.e., the night before writing this, I dreamed I was writing a poem. In the dream, I struggled to awaken so I could write down the poem but I could not. And I lamented like Tickle, on what was being lost because of my deep sleep. But struggle as I might I could not awaken.

This morning, I woke with the dream about a dream fresh in my head and the same sense of loss and a line, I think by Rimbaud, running through my head. 'The dead have dreams.' I was astonished to find paper scattered and that I had written something during the night, although of actually doing so I had no memory. This is what I had written:

> And praying only lasts while you've the need
> And sowing only lasts while there's a seed
> And hoping only lasts while there's chance
> And dancing only lasts the span of dance.
> The journey only lasts the length to go
> Fighting only lasts while you're the foe
> Talking only lasts while you've a voice
> And choosing only lasts while there's a choice

The singing only lasts while there's a song
And right would not be right without a wrong
And thinking's bound by chains inside your head
And dying lasts a lifetime, then you're dead,
But love goes on forever, a ceaseless circling river,
If there's any truth in what the gods have said.

I make no claims for it except that I think it is original. Certainly I don't think I've ever heard it before but, given my ability to block out things, who knows? For the moment, it's my own.

ANOTHER LIFE

I met an old friend in New York. Over three hundred years old. She was half-turned away from me, but I knew her as soon as I saw her, still wearing that fabulous yellow silk jacket trimmed with ermine and glimmering pearl eardrops; she was laying down her pencil to take a letter from another woman and had just put her hand to her chin in that way we all do when we are speculating on who might have sent the message.

A few months earlier, I went to see the Vermeer exhibition in The Hague. How did he paint like that? As though an angel in love with human beings and their humanity had painted them using some celestial pigment. But Vermeer was only a man, an artist with an incomparable way of seeing, who stared at a scene or a face, then looked at the canvas and transferred what he saw. It is what he made of what he saw – the reality of things – that matters. He blessed it, and we are blessed looking at it. Some of the images are confounding, in that you can't believe they were done with ground-up pigment, eggs, oil and turps; yet they do the opposite of confounding the spirit. They re-affirm truth, beauty, the intense valuableness of the everyday. They are all there, absolutely clear in the impeccable and glinting lights, yet what he did is as mysterious as life itself; there is a morality and a rigour to his vision that is glorious. He painted the poetic beauty of everyday life; there is seduction behind the old, shuttered facades, and anxiety and artfulness; but all take place in a world where verities are important – cleanliness, godliness, fortitude, industry, love; although the air glitters in the sun and the houses are sprinkled with sunlight, the only feelings are ones of tranquillity and quivering silence. That woman empties the basin into the trinket, the water flows towards the canal, and both children remain absorbed in their game, lambent and unthreatened forever. There is no outrage offstage, waiting at the traffic lights, shrieking around the corner. It's so simple I can't understand it.

Critics often write about the intensity of an artist's vision somehow suggesting a tunnelling process in which the artist gets to the true shape behind the thing being looked at. This is a matter of necessity for artists who come after an artist like Vermeer; they have to go to another place, since he saw what the world had to offer and what the reality of the world is worth. His pictures are so accurate as to be hallucinatory. So what's a chap like Degas, say, who comes long after him and who too loves life and the dailiness of things and can paint like an angel, to do? No use trying to repeat what Vermeer did even if he could; he or she has got to approach it – if that's the word – from a different place and a different angle. And artists do; they do, they do. There are plenty of analogies in music or literature. Take Austen and Joyce: both writing novels of manners, but the one doing the consummate thing a century before the other and so blocking all exits. So the later genius has to find another way. Which is easier said than done; he has to make a leap into a place without an atlas and, when he has landed and skidded to a halt, there is *Ulysses*. Well, *mutatis mutandis*.

What I can't believe when reading commentators and critics about Vermeer is their speculation about his anonymous sitters. Anonymous? There were never less anonymous people in their lives. They are a family called Vermeer and I don't mean in the circle of; I mean their surname was Vermeer and the woman he painted most often and with shining love is his wife. How do I know? If you were in The Hague and saw the pictures you would know too. The beautiful Mauritshuis Museum, more a little palace than a house, filled with devotional images, became a shrine during the exhibition. Many of the greatest are of a wonderful woman whom I insist is his wife. He painted her with such affection, knowledge and intimacy, doing her accounts, looking up from her desk, trying on a necklace, smiling at you as you enter her room for the first time. And every time she wears the same marvellous yellow silk jacket trimmed with ermine. This is the missus in her Sunday best. And, when I walked into the Frick Collection on East 70th Street in New York, there she was again; the Frick has three Vermeers, none of which was loaned to the great show, I don't know why, but I imagine it has to do with the terms of Henry Clay Frick's will.

The Frick is an amazing place, one of the greatest museums in the world, a steel magnate's monument to himself and his taste – and a man with a taste for symmetry. So, in his great hall, there are two Titians, one on either side of the great fireplace and two Hans Holbeins. Treasure follows treasure; not one but many paintings by Gainsborough, Bellini, El Greco, Turner, Rembrandt, Goya, Chardin, Corot, Van Dyck, not to mention whole rooms by Fragonard and Boucher; you become inured, accepting, unastonished; then, there, in the middle of the West Gallery, is 'The White Horse'. Constable once said, 'Painting is with me but another word for feeling', and, since he said about this painting, 'one of my happiest efforts on a large scale', you may imagine how this particular piece of extraordinary feeling shines out like a match struck in a dark room. He liked it so much he bought it back and kept it by him for the rest of his life.

I stood for a long time in front of it, looking at the shifty glaze of dark water, the way it turns to gleam, the two navvies straining to push forward the barge bearing the white horse, its great neck bowed in its greath, the tumble of clouds above the barn, the cows in the water stretching to nibble at the leaves above their head, the shadows, the meadows, the lanes. Arcadia. I was transported to a place I once knew but thought had vanished beyond any recall.

I had gone to New York to visit another exhibition entirely, a series of photographs taken by Diana Michener. She took many of the images in Dublin and lived with me, or in my house with me, while she was taking them. Every morning I watched her, with her long, balletic legs and small dark head, bicycling off into the wet Dublin day and I had an idea of what she was doing, also no idea. I saw some of the images, once, in a darkroom off Ladd Lane, just a glimpse soon after they were taken; pictures of absolute repose and absolute trauma that made me white with fear. They were even more unnerving in the context of a New York gallery; the show was described in *New York* magazine as 'the work of an artist searching for something that cannot finally be destroyed or corrupted – the spirit in the ruins of the flesh'. What I had seen cycling off was an absolute instrument tuned to what she was searching for. When she came home at night, she was still twanging; I scolded her for putting black socks into a white wash and you could see her brought down to earth, crash landing.

Between her images and the Vermeers and the Constable, I was in a place far away from New York, living an existence in other people's dreams and visions. Then I left the cool cloisters of the Frick and walked into the living hell of Fifth Avenue in gridlock, in a temperature in the high nineties, and remembered that New York has nothing to do with vicarious living. You can't be there and keep it a safe distance; even the most passive and depressed arrival is tugged into its pungent maw, given a good stir and sent out shaking, with a new nervous system. It peels itself for you, in-yer-face, come-and-get-it and I've noticed that, after a while, certain people begin to believe they are richer than they are, spend accordingly and go home penniless. Me, for example.

New York allows you to think you are the person you might have been. I'd come from a place where we'd been ruminating over the future (or lack of it) of a sixteen-year-old sheep called Pandora, who should have survived sixteen months at most but hung on for the rest of her life, halt, lame but lovable, and twenty-four hours later, I was prancing around Saks with a daisy cloche on my head so my daughter Daisy could see how it looked. I probably looked like Pandora but she didn't say a word.

I've always loved New York. I worked there for years, it was my town, my friends were there, I had the prettiest apartment on Fifth and East 88th Street, next door to the Guggenheim Museum founded by Peggy's uncle, and a few blocks up from the Metropolitan. I used to think, God forbid I would ever try to rear a family here. How would you do it? Never mind the financial constraints, think of the worry. And, suddenly, I had a family here and all my forebodings came true, plus something worse I'd never foreseen; I became ole Mrs Tagalong. Two daughters joined me, Daisy, lean and muscular, from the Argentine where she'd been riding for three months, and Bay from her university where she'd been writing about art and feminism, which gave her a certain armoury in dealing with young men with attitude.

They hit New York like two strong blue and green thunderbolts, flashes of acid transparent colour taking off down to SoHo and Chelsea to hang out with their friends. Where did they get all these friends, I asked myself wonderingly, How can this have happened?

How they and their friends dressed was, of course, the other reason I became Mrs-Out-Of-It; not because of the clothes necessarily, but because of the colours or rather the lack of them in my wardrobe. My old friend Joan Buck (well, not old, long-standing rather) now Editor-in-Chief of French *Vogue* (can you imagine an American taking French *Vogue* by the heels and shaking it into new vivid life – are the French ladies mad or what? Yes, raging) said she'd banned black from her magazine and 'telling women to buy black is like telling them to buy bread and milk'. Anyway, I looked like Mrs Corleone or somebody, an old immigrant relation schlepping around in the murk. And my daughters and their friends dressed entirely in colours we thought tacky, cheap, sleazy; electric blues and shiny purple, petrol greens and lime shimmer on their long narrow bodies. Walt Whitman, did he but know it, was the first fashion poet when he sang of the body electric. I am enchanted by the way they look, but I have no idea how to do it. I am going to learn. Pandora dressed as lamb.

Dressed up in these minuscule, day-glo garments, they go out night after night, having spent hours on the telephone arranging complicated rendezvous and drop-off points all over Manhattan; it seems impossible they will all meet up. I lie awake listening to the traffic on East 60th Street. It's six o'clock – seven o'clock in the morning and they're not back. My husband says, comfortingly, 'Don't fret, darling, they're hunting in pairs.' I don't know whether to be comforted or not and lie listening for the creak of the elevator.

As soon as I hear it start its long ascent, I know it's them, since no-one, save us, appears to be staying in this huge, ornate building, the Stanford White Club. The lift creaks. They are here like kingfishers in a glitter of brightness and make crooning, fluttering noises to show they are all right. They are not impatient that I have been worried but sympathetic. I listen; they went to the Tunnel, a night-club with Romeo, a hairdresser by day, a style king by night, then onto another salsa place uptown. Daisy says, 'I had to dance with a cook, a retard, and with a sailor who came up to my shoulder, while little Miss Cinders here is with the Prince talking about photo opportunities at *Vogue*; I'm salsa-ing with a man whose nose nestles at my knee and she's talking to Leonardo DiCaprio ...'

Night after night, they come back at three and four in the morning. It's my New York, but their friends are showing them a good time in a city I don't know, and I am suddenly in the business of remembering, and I don't like it. I like it when Constable reminds me; that kind of nostalgia is fine by me, but I don't like it when my own lifetime is fading into sub-fusc.

I cheer up in the mornings; we go cruising the great sights of New York; of course visit the Frick to tap into your own old heritage, your own sense of history and luxury. But tap into the stores to get a bead on how things look, how things look and feel *now*. But even here, the daughters show me a different world. I'd never go into a store like Diesel but Bay takes me; big noise, big bass, shiny, scummy-looking garments costing a lot but it's the label that counts. 'Forget Prada,' Bay says, 'I love Diesel.'

She tries on trashy-looking garments, nerdy shifts and, once on, they become gazzy and glitz and not so much chic (that old-fashioned word harking back to *Vogue* and grooming) as knife-edged, frosty, spare ... I leave her as she browses through acrid-coloured, kitsch, short-sleeved cardigans (in petrol green, yellow, orange at three hundred dollars a throw, things I'd have taken to the Oxfam shop in the seventies, I mutter to myself until I catch myself on and start wondering how I've got to be so wrong and when did I start sounding like my mother-in-law) and go to the coffee bar in the corner, with all the latest magazines, where a raving beauty behind the counter makes the best cappuccino and I think why can't shopping be like this in London and Dublin.

After an hour of serious trying-on (and after three days of shopping till she's dropping), Bay drifts over, looks at me seriously, draws in her breath and twists her face. A big thought is coming. Surely some revelation is at hand. 'I've lost my taste for shopping,' she says, then, in the same breath, says *sotto-voce* to Crystal, the assistant with caramel-coloured hair, by now her friend for life, who is clasping a purple jacket they both hanker after, 'Will you keep it for me and I'll think while I have a coffee?'

She joins me later with a large Diesel shopping bag; I don't question what's in it in case she tells me. We go to Bergdorf's, she stares at the Prada bags on the shelves with real longing. I note with interest they are seven hundred and fifty dollars. 'No,' she says, thoughtfully, 'I've changed my mind, there's still nothing like Prada.'

We go to Barneys on 59th and Madison and walk through one of the most beautifully crafted and lit spaces I have ever entered; each showcase is like a jewel; each counter a work of great design, each assistant by Fabergé. The whole, an immaculate temple to Mammon. I go to the make-up section to pick up the Trish MacEvoy make-up and Kiehl foundation I have been commissioned to buy by any number of friends in London and my eye is caught by an occurrence behind the glittering girl at the marble sales desk.

Nothing else in the store is moving. I realise the infinite, watery backdrop is an aquarium and the occurrence is an exquisite, dark fish shaped like a tear or Vermeer's pearl, the colour of a December evening sky, swimming around and around in its illuminated glass cage, with a sibilant, glistening loneliness. The fish seems wide-eyed and aghast, almost petrified at its fate as an accessory to the fact of artifice. Bay and I trail our fingers like fat snails across its glass cage and it noses along the invisible tracks looking out from behind its view into the painted, powdered world; it looks at us as though asking to be taken out and put back in the darkness, the deep darkness that matched those lambent eyes, wide open in the glare.

Suddenly, I am back in my old sense of the unreliability of New York, its way of using things for display and amusement and window dressing that should, by their nature, be beyond its reach: important things rendered frivolous. The very opposite of Vermeer.

A WINTER PALACE

S t Petersburg on a Saturday evening. I'd been told to expect size but this scale is beyond anything I've ever known. You sit in the middle of the square outside the Winter Palace and see, far, far away, a tiny figure, a lead-top soldier coming through an arch. Almost imperceptibly, it draws nearer and nearer, like something sinister being filmed by David Attenborough, then you see it's your husband out for a stroll across a town square. You sit open-mouthed at this townscape, the mixture of palaces and expanse of river, of onion-domed churches, baroque monuments and grand canals, all built on the whim of a visionary and on such a scale that paradoxically it is like looking at a great canvas by a Russian Canaletto, say, where everything huge and epic fits felicitously into a chosen vision. The Hermitage itself, its incomparable richness and vastness, are beyond fathoming; there is so much: Rembrandt after Rembrandt, English painting at its best, Impressionists on the grandest scale, the finest Matisses, the most exotic decoration, extraordinary furniture – you've only done a few rooms and there are hundreds more.

We were staying on a ship moored on the river. It's the safest place and, with only one gangplank entrance, there is a chance your clothes will still be in your wardrobe when you come back in the evening. On the other hand, you're in a suite the size of a biscuit box. It wasn't for reasons of safety or timidity that we were on a boat, but because we wanted to see both the great shimmering, wooden churches of Kizhi Island (miracles of construction out of the only building material at hand, the silver wood of the forest, twenty-two silver domes on one church alone), and to go right into Russia, to see the Russia Tolstoy and Chekhov wrote about, but most of all the country of Turgenev. To read Turgenev is to love the man and to fall in love with Russia. I always felt when reading about how Russians felt about their motherland that they had much in common with the Irish. That extraordinary passionate feeling, that love for the idea of a place so that even when they leave it, it shivers around them. His descriptions of the interior of the great country of Russia filled me with a yearning to see it.

I grew up in a landscape on a tiny scale. We thought Lough Neagh enormous, and murmured, with satisfaction, 'the biggest lake in the British Isles'; but all the same the lights of Lurgan were a close enough constellation at night and, in the other direction, there were the tiny fields of minuscule farms; the aerodrome was prairie to our eyes. I remember reading in an E.M. Forster novel about a group of picnickers spotting a figure appear over the line of the downs some five miles away and watching as he approached. The very concept of that untrammelled length of vision and view was baffling; as was the concept of the forty-acre field where the *Famous Five* or the *Secret Seven* or Wendy and Trix – English children of that ilk in those stories – would go and find buried treasures or dead spies. Where we lived forty acres was a big farm. In Turgenev you were introduced to a sense of space on a scale that was incomprehensible and beyond imagining. He makes the broad expanse of his native lands unroll before us in his books; forests, bushes, fields, ravines, plains, mountains, rivers, villages, churches, mossy swamps and lakes, always lakes. You fly over Russia in his company, the panorama unfolds below; the problem is that, if you fly over Russia now, you see nothing but cloud and your heart's in your mouth. So we were boating it.

As we boarded the boat that would take us up the Neva and across the two lakes into Northern Russia, a group of young women burst into warbling song. They were in white, shiny costume with embroidery – the kind of stab at national costume, done on the cheap, you sometimes see in productions of *The Gondoliers*. Our cabin was clean, large, comfortable and the colour of diarrhoea. Curious this insistence on trying to make plastic look like wood and, in the process, making it look like nothing on earth.

One of the details I particularly noticed about anything contemporary or new in St Petersburg was the meanness and crudity of most of the fabrics and materials used in their construction. I'm not talking about the restoration of the great monuments, the onion-domed churches, the sides of the canals, but about the things and stuff used in everyday living. It either looked cheap, shiny, gimcrack, or decaying and unpainted. At one point, while our group were wandering through a holy island, we met a group of inhabitants. We were all clad unobtrusively enough in linen and cotton in muted colours: slubs, drabs, white and faded blues; a boring lot you might say, so sub-fusc and decent; the Russians were clad in skimpy, shiny, carnival-coloured viscose. Such fabrics are not just worn by the rural poor: the costumes in the great Kirov ballet company at the Mariinsky were also tinsel, pinchbeck and synthetic colours. Before my last trip to New York, I would have said sagely, that the difference between a rich economy and a poor one is that the rich dress in natural fibres, the poor in synthetics, but in New York the young, with money to burn (relatively speaking), are recreating this very look from choice, while here it was a matter of expediency and poverty.

The boat moved off, while a band played, and Russian citizens, promenading along the quayside with their dogs and children, waved us goodbye, and we set off into this country that for so many years was a monolithic mass on the map. Talk about the heart of darkness. But, in fact, this country was entirely silver and green, the colour of the underside of a willow leaf, shimmering in the mist and the sun: this is the country of the white nights so that even at midnight, the world is silvered. The boat pulled long silver waves behind it; they seemed harnessed to the boat, breaking and shattering against low trees and shrubs on the bank but catching up again on the faint, taut tether of the ship's propeller.

On either side was mile upon mile of spectacular wood and forest. The wood, drenched with rain, kept changing its appearance as the sun shone out or went in behind the clouds. Sometimes it was all ablaze, as if everything there was smiling; the slender boles of the scattered birches suddenly took on the fresh brilliance of white silk, the tiny leaves on the ground gleamed and blazed with purple and gold, and the handsome stems of the tall curly bracken, already tinged with their autumn hue, the hue of over-ripe grapes, stood out luminously before me in an infinite, criss-crossed maze. Then suddenly the whole scene took on a faint shade of blue; in an instant, the bright colours went out, the birches stood blankly white as new-fallen snow, not yet touched by the cold light of the winter sun; and furtively, slyly, the finest of drizzles began to spray and whisper, trailing silver.

At one point, our boat was hoisted up through massive locks, their timbers straining. As we waited for them to fill, we met an Englishman who was working in the area trying to get a power station built and into production. He was just about to give up. The final straw came when he had eventually managed to get a load of timber for the construction sent up-river; it was loaded onto the *Rybinsk I*. Confident for once that things were on board and in hand, he went back to St Petersburg to try to organise the next batch of necessities. A week later, he got a telegram advising that no timber had arrived. Indeed, no boat had arrived. All had gone missing. Wearily, he set about tracking down an enormous, fully crewed boat that had vanished into thin air.

No-one knew anything, but the superintendent had interesting information. 'The ship sank,' he said.

'So where is the crew?'

'The ship sank with all hands.'

'The river has a draft of twenty feet,' Christopher said. 'It would be impossible to sink. Where was this disaster, this shipwreck, reported?'

'It was not reported, yes, but there are two, lovely, new, big, wooden *dacha* being built near to where it sank. Lovely big timbers.'

'Well,' Christopher said, 'we must get the police on to it.'

'One of the houses built belongs to a policeman.'

Later that year, a new boat appeared near the tragic spot on the river. It was in all respects exactly the same as *Rybinsk I*, except it had been newly painted and was now called *Rybinsk II*.

We slipped through the locks and entered an ocean of glittering water; hour after hour after hour, the waves tied to the boat silvered, endless; I have never seen such spaces. I ask the interpreter where we are, 'Here,' she says, her finger stabbing at a small blob of blue on the map. 'It could be one of two or three lakes but it is this one, Lake Onega.'

'How big is it?' I ask, looking up from the tiny lake tucked into a far corner of the map of this immeasurable country; I try to see the faintest hint of a smudge of land on the horizon.

'About the size of Ireland,' she says.

The next day, the boat docks at a place on the Svir river that is not on the itinerary. No-one dares question the captain. The interpreter is puzzled at this arbitrary, unscheduled tying-up of the big boat at a tiny pier in the middle of nowhere, but apparently the captain has taken to doing so on the last three cruises. We have been forewarned about this excitement so we all crowd the railings to watch the princely descent. A car comes out of the forest, the captain with a face that would set jelly, climbs in and disappears. We all speculate on the mystery. The consensus is that he has a new mistress. We don't care, we're delighted – the more mistresses the better, since it gives us an unexpected landfall. And lo, as we leave the ship and walk into the forest whose edges we have gazed at for so long, we come on a miracle. We find, intact, the Russia of our imagination, the Russia we know from Turgenev. Beautiful, squalid houses lie low around a mirror lake; there are no fences; the fields run to the water's edges; silver birch groves reflected in the still water. And birds singing so loudly that each note falls, plop into the water, like Caruso shattering glass. We feel shy at its beauty.

It is like stepping into a medieval illustration from one of the *Très Riches Heures*. Everything so contained and beautiful, but the faces of the older Russians are dull, low-browed and look poverty-stricken. As we walked, the wild flowers were astonishing; peonies and campanula, delicate and fervent, an extraordinary yellow orchid, a briony with purple leaves and yellow flowers, a colour no-one would imitate in life, sweet vernal grass, purple moor grass, reed grass, field horsetail, all kinds of flowering rushes and thistles – the marsh thistle, the meadow thistle; sedges, wild scabious and carnations, vetchling and bird's foot trefoil, clovers and many more I could not recognise. But what made it unique and startling was the setting itself, the lack of noise, the lack of road penetrating its organic unity. It is the through-traffic that has ruined England and most places in Western Europe. Every village is bisected by roaring traffic, tearing in and roaring out, having driven a noise-wedge through the village and invested it with impermanence. Everywhere is only another place on the way to somewhere else. It disturbs everything – harmony, pace, rootedness. I seem not to have been born with the screening filter that makes you cut out on noise or audibility. Everything comes in like a buzz-saw and it makes life very difficult. Here there was no noise. The blessed peace of not hearing the internal combustion engine – that's what we've lost by giving in to the car; the peace and organic feeling. I hope I am right in thinking that, in twenty or thirty years' time, roads will go under or around towns – no villages left – but that is not the same. This village, slumbering by the lake, seemed completely self-contained.

We went for a walk across a low island, with occasional wooded inclines dissected by small gleaming streams. There were bridges every few yards across these little rivers and pools. Dotted on the wild slopes were farm houses which reminded me with poignancy of the farmhouses of my childhood. Unkempt, manure heaps near the doors, ploughs and carts lying where they had been unharnessed, animals living in close proximity to the humans, sometimes under the same roof, livelihood and life mixed together, with squalor and the way of life that endured before the arrival of the conveniences that made life cleaner: here, there was no electricity, no machines. As we walked over a bridge and towards where the river curled away on a bend, we heard a savage noise in the distance. A crazed, livid, continual, high screaming, and when, frightened and alarmed, we found where the noise was coming from, we saw this terrible tableau. A woman with huge, bare knees, the scoured turnip face that so many old women seem to have in Russia, a headscarf over her scant hair, hands rising and falling in pain, and around her, squatting or kneeling, stroking or patting her, four other people. Her mouth was open and she was screaming, keening, wailing, bewailing, her heart already broken, and we, listening to her, felt ours fit to break.

We turned away, ashamed to be tourists at such a scene. The whole day was skewered by her grief. When we got back to the boat, we learned that, the previous day, a group of tourists had found a child's body floating there in a shallow pool. This was the mother, sitting at the spot where her four-year-old's body had been laid.

In the distance, we saw the captain's car driving back to the boat and we hurried back to its haven, its sleek lines, its conveniences, its air conditioning, our space capsule, scooping up its aliens, leaving behind the ravening noise and the void.

On board, the interpreter told us that the mystery of the unscheduled stop had been solved. The captain was supervising the building of a *dacha* in the nearby village. I didn't ask where the timbers had come from, and I tried not to think of the child running across the bridges, through the pools ... as we steamed towards the silver churches through the long white Russian night, I stayed on deck a long time.

HOLDING ON

'Show me your cupped hands,' Gudrun said. This I did.

We both stared into the little tarn. Black, bottomless. Not just inky fingers, blackened palms, but hands like things that had been buried in peat, Tollund woman's hands. I still use a fountain pen to write and the ink seems to seep osmotically up, up, up towards my arteries.

After her first frightened glance she, being impeccably mannered, didn't otherwise remark on the blots and stains, the palimpsest of my writing day. 'You have tiny hands,' she said.

'I know,' I said, all complacency. 'I'm a princess at heart; or an old queen by now, like so many in Dublin.'

'Think of that little hollow as your stomach,' she said. 'That's its size.' Now, whenever I am faced by revelation, I start to gabble. Paul fell off his horse when he saw the light, I become a rattle.

'Because I have small hands?' I said. 'Or are all stomachs small? Are all stomachs the same size? Or if I had enormous hands would I have an enormous stomach like men with big noses are supposed to have enormous ...' I stopped. 'Goodness, I have teeny little hands,' I said, to cover myself. I was also seriously in love with the little blackened hand-hollow by now, although I found it hard to give credence to Gudrun's revelation. My stomach had obviously never been told what size it was meant to be. Indeed, I think my adorable little stomach suffers from the same disease as do the many people who think they have a problem with their body. We think it must be bigger to survive. It not only wants to be large and round, it *needs* to be, and, with seven miles of intestine lumbering and tumbling around it, who can blame it? In fact, come to think of it, the stomach is a very good metaphor for a woman's lot. It has to take in whatever is pushed at it, keep the whole thing going and send it out all tidied up, at the same time trying to keep itself neat, small and flat, whilst living in a heaving jungle of pipes and wires and waterworks and mains connections; and, most of all, it has to take in and give out nourishment.

When I lived in New York, my BF was Jean Shrimpton. I used to watch Jean's eating habits with fascination. We would order the same meal but, after a while, she appeared to lose interest in her food and to abandon it. I know now I was wrong in my analysis. She never had any interest in the food in the first place, or no more interest than I would have, say, in slaking my thirst with water. A couple of swigs and you're there; you don't want any more. But food for People Like You and Me (let's call them PLUMs for short) is often something more than nourishment. PLUMs do not look on food as meals, which are nourishment. Meals are events that occur in the day like any other event and, on the whole, PLUMs eat them normally, perhaps more, perhaps less, than anyone else, but there is no radical difference. *Food* is quite different; PLUMs are connected to food in a way that thin people do not comprehend, and it has nothing to do with being greedy. It is a life-line and, for PLUMs, food fills some void that has nothing to do with normal physical hunger. Some people would immediately say it was to do with sex and fright and, no doubt, in some cases, it has. What surprises me is how, with all the knowledge we now have about psychological disorders and abuse, being overweight is still treated as a cosmetic thing when in so many cases it is a nervous illness, a pathological condition, hard to treat and hard to cure. Because there seems to be an obvious and simple remedy – keeping your mouth shut – it is regarded as an easily solvable problem.

Not so. It is horribly difficult. Those who do not suffer from this condition think it has to do with willpower or the lack of it. Such people often evince far fewer signs of willpower in the areas where they have their own problems than overweight people, who, I've noticed, are frequently perfectionists and achievers in everything except in their own, often helpless, refusal to conform to the standard. The person who refuses at a most profound or subconscious level to do something that seems simple – i.e., command the mouth to stay closed – is, at the conscious level, trying desperately to countermand that refusal. They are trying to say no to food; but the other part, the stronger part, but also the part that is out of their control, is refusing to collude, and is saying yes, yes, yes, not to food, but to comfort (or consolation) in the form of food. One of my theories is that a person with a chronic weight problem has had too many real refusals and deprivations at a time when he or she was powerless, and the psyche not only will not buy into the deal ever again but seeks steadily to compensate.

Have you ever noticed how people without a weight problem say they can eat what they like – and then don't? And people with a problem say they can't eat what they like, then do? And, you think about it, if you can't eat what you like, then you've already created a problem. Denial brings its own refusals.

Anyway Gudrun, my Swedish guru, in a defining moment,

looked at my cupped hands and told me this amazing piece of news about what I thought was a huge, ravening monster that needed to be kept at bay at all times. (Defining moments are when someone says something that subtly, inoffensively, nudges your vision onto a slightly different skew. Such moments are rare enough.)

I have observed that people who have weight problems have generally not had emotional constancy in their life. They generally do not trust people. Being overweight brings a good deal of wretchedness to most. This is a truism and the corollary is – if it makes you wretched why do you continue to bear the burden; and, at some level, the reason must be that we must want or seek the wretchedness. Not, perhaps, at a perceptible level, but at some profound out-of-reach way. We are all educated enough in the reasons for child abuse to know that, for some, the only ratification of love is when the abuse is repeated. These dark circles are hard to break.

At a meeting of women where weight was an issue, someone said, 'We all like being fat.' There were howls of protest, of anguish. She wasn't being an *agent provocateur*, she was speaking what she saw as the truth, and I was inclined to agree with her. If we don't love being fat, why do we hold onto it so dearly that if we do lose it we want to claw it back? Because the true person you are is buried effectively? Not true. Because only you have access to yourself when you're fat and the fat will be the shield to ward off the difficulties of life? Not true. Because you opt out of the competition? Not true. Because you are comfortable with yourself? Usually not true. Yet many of these are real reasons even if they are not true and, in that gap between reason and truth, is the space where people with weight problems founder. All being overweight does is make life more difficult, not just in terms of fashion and health, but in how people regard and perceive you.

Every so often, I get thin. I like it. I look better, I wear pretty clothes – Prada, Polo, Dolce & Gabbana things, such stuff as I'd never dream of getting for myself but acquire in a darksome ritual called Nicking from the Daughters. When I'm thinner, I can't imagine feeling and looking any other way. I look with horror on the idea of putting the pretty clothes back into their wardrobes (no, I tell a lie, into their clothes heaps) and going back to the sub-fusc. Yet a year or two later, it has happened. It is as though someone is waiting behind a door through which I must walk, and, as I enter, that malign shadow drops an integument over me so I am blind and powerless and feeling my way into the world again and I must have my protection. Yet in every other way, I am a rational enough person. The ailment goes shockingly deep.

Now, if you are not a PLUM, if you do not have this problem, you will not comprehend what I am saying; you will think, impatiently no doubt or more likely complacently, it is my fault. It has nothing to do with fault or, if it has, then it is the same fault alcoholics and gamblers have. In finding solutions and forswearing guilt and blame, you have to search for clues within yourself, listen to yourself, give yourself some of your own time. Again, I have observed that PLUMs often have a lot of time for others and their needs and not a lot for themselves. You have to take your clues where you find them; when earlier, I mentioned the Nicking of the Daughters' Clothes, I said I would never dream of buying these clothes myself. And why not? Because I don't deserve them? I don't think so. In fact, I think I'm the *most* deserving case for anything going. Because I can't afford them? Too rational. Anyway I buy furniture and paintings I can't afford all the time. But one thing I have learned is that rationality has little to do with the problem. It lies at some deep inchoate level which takes a lot of work to reach; people often talk about 'going on a diet' – dread words – in the same way they talk about giving up smoking; they know they will give up only when they truly want to give up – until then it's no use – and then they will fight the addiction. But food isn't a dangerous drug and, when smokers give up, they give up completely and, if you do that with food, you die; we all know about anorexics now, but, when I was growing up and was severely anorexic at school, no-one knew anything about it so the problem was compounded. Indeed, the problems so many adolescents face and which we carry on into womanhood are underlined and underwritten by the images we see every day.

The truth is women are built to be heavier than the current beauty ideals; unrealistic standards are set for us all the time. For decades, women have been presented with the image of an ideal which has almost nothing to do with their own reality. Twenty years ago, models were ten per cent thinner than the average woman; now they are twenty-three per cent thinner. Almost a quarter less. For me, the nadir was reached when Twiggy and her ilk became the icons; androgynous, pre-pubescent pre-women, as it were. Women have enough demands made on them without being presented with almost unassailable images of their sex, locked into a time-warp somewhere before menstruation and maturity. No wonder young women become tentative, begin to hate their developing breasts and hips. It's hard to operate without models when you're young and you just don't have the self-confidence not to want desperately to conform. I'm not even going to bother with the moral implications. We become obsessive because we are suppressing and fighting our natural needs and desires and eating becomes a form of warfare. Many women look and feel guilty in restaurants when they order food they like. Men simply don't react the same way.

Gudrun has helped me a good deal and her advice is simple; she didn't tell me much that was new; the irony is that anyone who has a problem with his or her weight is generally more of an expert about food than most doctors. We all know that, if we listened to our body hunger and really fed it – the poached egg on lettuce, the grilled fish – we wouldn't have a weight problem. Sensible eating, old hat stuff and boring; but so hard to do consistently and over a long period. Many people with a weight problem rise up in the morning, full of good intent, and are amazed at their lack of willpower the evening before. Gudrun pointed out that I have low sugar levels and, by six o'clock, my metabolism is crying out for something sweet. Eating a banana stills the craving. A simple thing, but beyond me before she came along. She also pointed out that, far from wanting exercise, at certain times the body is crying for a rest. Sitting down and listening to music or simply doing nothing, i.e., not being busy, is a task beyond most women.

There is also something very basic you can do: go to a nutritionist and find out what minerals and vitamins your body lacks. Many nutritionists believe that the Irish and the Scots have a predisposition towards craving fat foods because of their cultural and social history; they will also tell you simple and revealing things such as that most of us don't drink anything like enough water and that, for every cup of coffee you drink, you need two and a half cups of water to flush it out.

Well, I've given myself a year to follow her advice, take all her vitamins and stare long and hard into the little cupped palms. By then, I intend to have turned into Emily Dickinson, wraith-like, frail, white-robed, beating my wings against poetry.

THE RESCUE OPERATION

*L*ast week I was having one of those periodic culls, the annual ritual of the Throwing Out of Things. Thank God for jumble sales, those vast, soothing depositories for left-overs. In one of the store cupboards (it resembles Madison Square Garden during a bad bout), I unearthed a doll, a beautiful simulacrum of a baby. I remembered it well and, indeed, why I had kept it – it was neither in good enough repair for the perfectionist childmums who like dolls, nor quite broken enough for me to jettison easily. So there it lay, mutely delivering messages about limbo until I was overcome by this annual lust for purge, to jettison junk. But, as everyone except the purists among us knows, when you start to try to throw away, rubbish can suddenly acquire an exquisitely sentimental value and the more I threw out, the more I clawed back a moment later. At last in a fit of stern resolve, I seized on the doll as the token sacrifice and slung it in an arc towards the dustbin; it somersaulted, a hiccup or whimper issued from its innards and, as it hit base, the impact kick-started the whimper into a familiar melody. I scrabbled among the detritus and rescued the creature, which instantly fell silent. I smacked it to see if I could produce its melodious death rattle again.

My little nephew observed all this with grave and pleased interest. He thought a surrogate smack-object was very good news. 'Perhaps,' he said hopefully, 'you should take it by the neck and wiggle it like a dog.'

This I did, while pondering on who exactly he was acquainted with that wiggled dogs by the neck, and found, embedded in the doll neck, a key which started a music box located in its stomach. It tinkled into Brahms' 'Lullaby', which, in its English version, is known – or is certainly known to me – as 'Rose's Whisper'. For years I sang it every night to my daughter Rose, and she, naturally enough, thought it composed specially for her. The song and my singing had been woven into the memory of years now gone. Indeed, if she hears me singing now, she howls with laughter or pretends she has never seen me before. All the same I listened to this melody with lachrymose interest and thought to rescue the little turnkey intestine as a symbol and souvenir.

I told Tom, 'I'm going to cut Rose's whisper out.' I laid the doll out on the chopping-board and got down the cleaver, a fearsome-looking instrument in the shape of a stalking wolf, its extended tail being the handle, a most pataphysical instrument and, humming the melody, set to work, brandishing the cleaver and dismembering the doll.

You have, I trust, absorbed the scene. The kitchen is full of your usual images – dried flowers and smoked, wrinkled things (mostly me), ancient dressers groaning under old china, picked up not for the proverbial song but for a fairly weighty aria; in one corner, perched high on the arm of a chair, a cat cleans itself thoroughly, beneath it the white bull terrier lies patiently, waiting for the cat to fall so that he may savage it; I am bent over my butcher's block, hacking up a doll, swinging the cleaver, between grunts humming Brahms' 'Lullaby'.

It is Lizzie Borden time down Somerset way, the plastic torso is resilient and intractable and, under the blows, the musical box gives an occasional little tinkle. My little nephew is very pleased; he was particularly cross about not being allowed to see *Pulp Fiction*. After a particularly savage rise and fall of the axe, I comprehend a different quality to the noises in the kitchen, a sub-text to the bull terrier's patient pantings. It is the silence that comes when someone is keeping very quiet, no sudden movement. Every mother or aunt distrusts that silence to her bones, but this silence was not to do with children. My nephew was still riveted to the spot.

I look up, cleaver poised, and see, standing in the doorway, my friend and, just behind her, staring over her shoulder, mouth slightly open, the man about whom she has mooned and dreamt for a long time – the new young doctor in the local surgery. She is trying to nudge him back out of the room, but he wants to see if he is seeing what he thinks he is seeing.

'We were just driving to Stourhead so I thought I'd drop in so you could meet Edward,' she says, her tone bright and tight. Her eyes are starting from her head; *his* eyes are riveted to the butcher's block. In an instinctive action, I put down the axe and wipe my hands down my apron, and both sets of eyes follow the movement as though to look for the great red tracks my hands must leave behind.

'I've told him so much about you,' Jane says.

His eyes are on the axe and torso locked on the block like something out of the Black Museum in Scotland Yard. He doesn't speak.

I say, with desperate goodwill, 'It's so nice to meet you. You're the new doctor. You'd know with all your training how to help me tear this apart? I'm looking for Rose's whisper.'

Afterwards, as I rescued the cat from the bulldog and wriggled it a bit to punish it for falling, I said to Tom, who was rattling the mangled torso, 'Tom, who do you know who wriggles animals by the neck?'

'I don't know nobody except you,' he said very, very loudly. No. I lie. He shouted it and went out of the kitchen carrying the Crippenesque object.

Later that day, my sister came to collect Thomas who could not be parted from the Terrible Torso. My sister, being kind, did not ask any questions, but, all the time we were saying goodbye, Tom kept up the terrible, loud, roaring noise, shouting his goodbyes, and nothing would make him stop. 'Talk louder, Mum,' he urged her. 'Talk louder.'

Later my sister telephoned. 'Why can't we whisper any more?' she asked.

'Hello?'

'Why can't we whisper? That's why Tom was shouting all the time we were leaving. He was frightened to lower his voice. He said that if you whisper in your house you cut the whisper out.'

INITIATORY DRAWINGS

A friend of mine has a little Neapolitan watercolour. When I enquired of its provenance, he said he'd bought it at the selling-up sale of Glyde Court. I stared at it for the longest time.

In life you come across things that puzzle you, disproportionate to their importance or relevance. Well, I do; every so often, an old mystery slurps up out of the murk of the mind – not necessarily old-fashioned mysteries like the *Marie Celeste* abandonment, the Bermuda Triangle or Uri Geller, things that under rational examination turn out to be more or less explicable, nor those mysteries closer to home like why you constantly lose your keys when you know you need them or why you continue to behave in ways that damage you – these mysteries are dynamics in life; at best some sort of repair is going on, at worst, some repetition of early damage. Nor am I talking about those things which, in my childhood, were called mysteries of faith, to question which was to question the whole foundation of the system of belief by which we lived. Well, this is what faith is; credulity, unquestioning belief. Night after night, we recited the five glorious mysteries, the five sorrowful ones, and I forget the rest because I don't want to remember. It all seemed darkish to me and, in any case, I couldn't see anything so mysterious about the Crowning with Thorns or the Carrying of the Cross, they seemed all-too-clearly fathomable examples of man's inhumanity to man.

I've always disliked mysteries; they add to the chaos that stands ready to engulf us. I like things that are explicable, plain and withstand scrutiny. I remember reading, in de Tocqueville's letters from Ireland, a sentence spoken to de Tocqueville by an old priest in 1832, 'The Protestants hold that we love the dark. They will soon see that we love the light.' But, over a hundred years later, we still lived in the dark or, at least, that is how I saw it in my childhood; life lay in an old murkiness.

Of course, a great deal of this apprehension of the darkness of early days is because the lights weren't switched on, literally. Until I was in my mid-teens, the rooms of all the houses I knew were lit by lamps or candles. The prevalence of artificial light is one of the greatest changes that has taken place in my lifetime. No-one born since the sixties in Ireland can know how dark everything was for a great many months of the year. The nights closed in so early and each room was lit by oil lamps, later by pressure lamps called 'Tilleys', which burned with an alarming, sudden incandescence. In our house we were well advanced, in that all the rooms on the ground floor were lit by gas lights, with little dangly chains with 'Off' and 'On' filigreed into discs which had been put on the wrong way round; I still have difficulty with didactic instructions on containers and labels since the reverse always appeals to me. The mantles were fragile, white objects like wasps' nests or fretted meringue, which shattered at a touch. They were the most delicate things I'd seen outside the artifacts of nature.

I was mystified by the idea that such a little confection could survive the journey from the factory to the shop to our house in its rural fastness, made as the mantles were of cotton or artificial silk, saturated in a chemical solution, and burnt to crispness. The type of mantle we used had been invented in Austria only a decade or so before it was installed in our house; and, in retrospect, I am surprised by the speed of its adoption and installation in houses in Ireland, considering the bulk of the gas containers, the intricacies of installing the system; it burned with a lovely glow, much softer than the electric bulb. The 'electric' came to our district only in 1957, and, suddenly, there was illumination everywhere, and, as though a torch had been held up to an old fresco, corners you had never seen before showed up their detail.

The lights of Lurgan had always been a kind of glimmering girdle on the other side of the pitch black expanse of the lough, sometimes glistening in the path of the moon. The rich, velvety, indecipherable darkness of the sky has long since disappeared from the skies in the western hemisphere. Reflected light from the world's illuminations has rendered our night sky much lighter than ever in our history; the stars are disappearing under the onslaught of sodium lights from our cities.

One night in 1957, driving back from Lurgan, we could see, for the first time, light on our side of the lough. So as quickly as that, over the span of one day, we jumped from a medieval existence of darkness to one where, at the flick of the switch, not only was all darkness banished, but, at the flick of another, we entered the new, alien, outside world of television, a luminous, ectoplasmic, plague-spreading infection, destroying the recipe for being a community. Was it at that time that October Devotions stopped?

Those were magical, mysterious evenings walking to and from the chapel in the autumn darkness. The mystery came not from the Devotions inside the little dark chapel but from the quick brightness of the stars above us, the spilled stretch of the Milky Way and the Cassiopeia cluster. We watched for shooting stars, since this meant there had been a displacement in the firmament through which a soul had entered heaven. All along the road made so mysterious by the darkness, we could see the black outline of couples or groups of people, walking towards the chapel, silhouetted against the silvered skyline; on each side of the dark hedges, in the middle of many fields, stood a fairy thorn undisturbed for centuries.

Life was more mysterious then, people looked odder, things were kept concealed, there was no merit to frankness; book learning was easy to come by, but there wasn't much street wisdom about, or, if there was, I could not tap into it. I remember at boarding school, at the end of the summer term, a group of older girls began an endless whispering, but, when any of us younger ones came near, they stopped. One of the older girls took pity on us and promised to reveal the secret at the beginning of the September term. It was unimaginable but true that, as we sang 'O Causa Nostra Laetitiae', the holiday hymn, I longed for the holidays to be over before they had started. Alas, I never returned to that school and now the secret will never be revealed; like the one about Fatima which haunted all our childhoods and which the Pope was supposed to reveal in 1960. Then, when it came to the crunch, he didn't. So it hangs in there still like a rennet bag.

All this train of thought about mysteries was brought on by the Glyde watercolour; Glyde Court was a Georgian house (with nineteenth-century Jacobean additions to romanticise it up) in county Louth, where the Vere Foster family lived. In the National Gallery in Dublin there is a fascinating portrait by Sir William Orpen of members of the family – the epigone, you might say – painted in 1907. This portrait seems to reveal the absolute necessity of separateness as a means to sanity and, though it appears to be such a conventional picture of an upper-class family, almost a piece of iconography, it is full of mystery. You can hardly take your eyes off Sir Vere, with his red kerchief hanging out of his pocket, his rakish bow tie, those anxious eyes in the etiolated face. He is all accessory, and beside him stands the ultimate accessory, his wife Lady Foster, looking like a contemporary *Vogue* model in taupe, beside them their two daughters, extremely got-up and ravishingly pretty, one in lace and furbelows, the other a dead ringer for one of the doomed Princes in the Tower. I love this picture on its own account, but I stare at it because I know so many more important facts about the occupants of those painted bodies than they themselves knew; my account is the final tally. I know for example that, long after the picture was painted, Lady Foster did what many of us want to do, but she did it to excess. She hibernated all winter – never got out of bed. I know that the nine-year-old girl who looks like the Prince, a dandy to her fingertips, went on to re-christen herself John, wore a tie and a man's hat, cropped her hair, wore breeches, a fantasy that arose, as it so often does, from the desire to fulfil her mother's wish for a son and heir. I know that sometimes the donkey, with its burden of dead birds, had to be painted in the drawingroom as it rained every day of that summer when Orpen was painting the portrait – which the Fosters at first liked but later grew to dislike. In that year, 1907, Orpen lived in the same chiaroscuro gloom in which we, fifty years later, lived.

I know all this, but, most of all, I know what they couldn't know, that another child, Anthony, was to be born to this gilded, haunted couple. Anthony sounds like a character out of a Molly Keane novel – light-hearted, marvellous, with a capacity for joy, but with the undertow of melancholy pulling him down. He revived the Midsummer Festival of Pattern or Patrun in Tallanstown near Glyde. (I wonder if the festival is still held there

at midsummer?) I can never look at this portrait without
remembering what Mark Bence-Jones wrote in his witty and
remarkable book, *Twilight of the Ascendancy*; it invests the portrait
with extraordinary significance and a sense of *lacrimae rerum*. He
wrote about the boy whose invisible future presence stirs beneath
the surface of this picture: 'Later that year [1934] his regiment
moved from India to Khartoum where, in September, he was
found dead in tragic and mysterious circumstances.'

Deconstructionists might disapprove, but that elegiac
sentence colours my whole view of the picture. What, I wonder,
were the tragic and mysterious circumstances? Perhaps, like the
secret in the playground, you know the answer in your bones; best
to let it lie there. The other thought that crosses my mind when I
look at that picture is what I would have been like if, in childhood,
I had been dressed up like either of those children. Could you ever
get over it? A whole generation and class of English children never
got over their grounding in class consciousness through clothes.
And not only English – I once read that Rilke's mother pretended
he was a girl until he was five, called him 'Sophie' and refused to
cut his ringlets. Forever afterwards he could never abide living
with anyone, though he loved women to distraction. He was a
genius of course. His poem 'Panther', which begins, 'this gaze
those bars keep passing is so misted with tiredness, it can take in
nothing more,' is stunning. For pure force only 'Tyger Tyger' by
Blake can pad along with it.

I was pondering on the Vere Foster portrait and wondering
why the name was so utterly familiar when I remembered – how
could I have forgotten? – it was indeed as familiar as my own
handwriting. When we were children at Moortown Public
Elementary School all our copying and drawing books were called
'Vere Fosters'. All our letters were drawn under the guidance of
his name, our first attempts at joined-up letters were drawn by

following his printed examples and our drawings – Initiatory Drawings (I used to wonder what an Initiatory was) in Domestic Objects (Simple) and Domestic Objects (Perspective) were done under his aegis. And, indeed, the Sir Vere Foster of this portrait, thirty-four at the time he was painted, was the great-nephew of the philanthropist and educationalist who invented these copy books used by generations of Irish school children; one way or another, he taught us all how to write.

So I wish I too had been at the selling-up of the contents of Glyde Court. I'm not in the business of souvenirs and mementoes but I would have liked something to cherish this family by, these mysterious people I know so well and knew not at all.

SUNDAY MORNINGS
IN THE COUNTRY

Only Johnny reading the Sunday papers could find innuendo after innuendo, which he read out with raised eyebrows and a hurt, astonished look, his brown eyes full of mischief. He knew that fear is the enemy of love; but he had lived half his life unloved, in a state of fear, manifestly homosexual when it was against the law to be so. He fell in love with the man he went to work for, who fell in love back.

He used to come and stay with me on occasional weekends, especially after his partner died. My children adored him, so did Olive who was eighty and ran the house with a rod of putty. I loved listening to Johnny. Coming from Ireland not long before, I had never met that cast of mind, never come across that form of defence called 'camp'. He was bereft but he was never miserable and he had innocence and unquenchable gaiety and a sense of life's silliness; give him a book or a newspaper and he became a dowser, his mind a divining rod quivering over good, clean, often boring, articles on poetry, cookery, travel; in the most erudite text he could delve into a magma of scatological references and *double entendres*. 'One track mind, dear,' he would say. 'No terrible diversions like you have with these poppets.'

I can see him now.

We were in the drawingroom. It was Sunday morning, just before lunch, and two of my children were absorbed in a book, golden heads soldered together as in a whimsical nursery illustration and I, bewildered by this sudden, good, strange silence, was speculating on what they could be reading to rivet them so, but held my peace. Johnny was impressed.

'Penises,' Rose said loudly. 'There.' A finger jabbed at the book. 'Spelt like peanuts only with the T out.' Daisy was *bouleversé* at such learning. I didn't look at Johnny, who slowly lowered his paper to goggle over at the two nymphets and then at me. I saw they had found a manual called *Where Did I Come From?* which a well-meaning friend once brought them under a Liberty cover. (Looking at it now, twenty years later, I note with surprise it was written by Peter Mayle when Provence was surely only a twinkle in his little eye.)

'Where did *it* come from, you might ask,' Johnny said.

'It tells you here,' said Rose, dimpling at him. 'You've got one of those peanut things, haven't you, Johnny?'

Rose is what Olive calls 'not safe'.

'Last time I checked I had,' he said, and looked across at me.

I lowered my face slowly onto the table. Ostrich syndrome. 'It's you,' I said, my voice muffled into the tablecloth. 'It's your influence.'

'Not me, duckie,' he replied. 'I've never seen that book before in all my life. It was here before I got here. But I must look at it. It might teach me something by the sound of it. Better than *this* anyways.' He rattled the newspaper. 'And this is supposed to be the saucy one. Let's see, girls,' he said. 'Show and tell.'

'No,' Rose and Daisy said firmly, 'we're using it.' They tittered horribly. Unfazed, he returned to his paper, and I looked at the children who, pleased to have my attention, pounced.

'Mummy, what's C-L-I-?' Rose began. I raised my head from its pillow of shame and met Johnny's eyes, gazing at me with interest.

'Go on, dear, do tell. Cling film, perhaps?'

'No,' Rose said. 'Not cling. It's C-L-I-T-'

'Say no more,' Johnny said. 'Spare your mother's blushes. There are but two words in the English language beginning like that so it must be the raised band encircling the body of earthworms towards the middle.'

'Oh, come on, Johnny,' I said. 'You've made that up.'

'On my life,' he said.

Rose wrinkled her nose in disgust. '*Worms,*' she hissed at Daisy.

'Stop it, Johnny,' I said. 'Think of the appalling word-associations you're giving that child.'

'Talking about encircling the body,' Johnny said, 'why don't we go upstairs and try on that shantung suit you say you're chucking out. I can't think why.'

'It will suit you,' I said.

'It will suit my florid complexion more like,' he said.

Underneath his face and body, the lineaments of the young, unhappy boy he had been years and years before were almost perceptible. He tried the jacket on and said, posing, vamping it up, 'I knew I was – well, 'gay' you call it now, but there was nothing gay about it then, I can tell you, 'queer' it was called and queer you felt – when I was fourteen. I didn't admit it until I was about twenty-two, of course; and I still think it's a fairly hideous joke on the part of Nature.'

'How did you know?' I asked.

'Well, all the boys were after girls, they never stopped talking about it and I hadn't the faintest interest. Didn't know what they were talking about.'

'What did you do?' I asked.

'What could I do? I thought I was sick, wrong, gone mad. It was so different then. Everything was closed, fearful, inhibited. There was no-one to ask then and nothing to read, nothing to do except worry yourself sick. Then I became a Bevin Boy. You don't know what that is, I can see – shows your age, you're so young.'

'I'm not, Johnny,' I said. 'I'm not.'

He looked at me consideringly. 'Well then, I'm so old. It was during the war. Bevin Boys were conscripts sent to essential industries ... docks, mines. I'd been on the colliery anyway, the wages desk, and then was called up and went into the Pay Corps. I was sacked from that – suspected TB – and I thought after the colliery there simply *must* be more to life than this, perhaps I could be a factotum of some kind. So I put an advertisement in the paper. It was extraordinary how many answers I got. I only answered one. A doctor who'd gone blind: I honestly thought I could do some good. He was a poppet. She was a real bitch – kept a coat of arms in the hall showing she was descended from William the Conqueror, well, weren't we all? Although I was very unhappy, I stayed there quite a long time because I thought I was helping. But it got too much and by chance – well, not chance, call it Fate – I'd kept one address from all those letters. I wrote and the man asked me to come for an interview. It was too long a journey for a day so I stayed overnight. There were flowers in my room and cigarettes and I thought it was perfect heaven.'

'It was perfect heaven,' I said. It had been a most beautiful house with Johnny at its happy centre and, since his friend had died, Johnny was a walking metaphor for bereavement. (But he was so gallant; it was one of the reasons we all loved him.)

He came downstairs and went over to the piano and played 'Linden Lea', quite without pathos in his jauntiness. He stopped the music. 'I hate being alone. For all the clichéd reasons. There are always good reasons for things being clichés. The coming home at night to an empty house. Not being able to turn to someone and say "Look" when there is something beautiful you want to share ... all that. But I knew I'd end up alone. Always. I believe in Fate. Predestination. I don't know how to reconcile it with my Christianity; I go to church every Sunday – drive seven miles because the pastor there is a human being. His sermon last Sunday – he was saying how he'd been swimming off the coast, at Formentor. My dear, he's eighty-four, and he was swamped by a wave – well, to look at him a bit of foam would knock him over – and he lost his teeth. There he is in the pulpit, describing the loss of his dentures. He searched everywhere and eventually gave up and went back to his hotel; toothless and *minding*, you could hear how he minded, and wouldn't you? On holiday? It takes ages to replace them at the best of times, and eighty-four or not, you don't want that awful, sudden sag – and he couldn't eat. He went out for a walk and, when he came back, there they were, in a parcel, on his place. If that isn't a miracle, what is?'

He pushed aside the paper and lifted a book by Harold Acton. 'More confessions I see. You've got catholic tastes. But then you are, aren't you?'

'When I lived in Tuscany,' I said, showing off, 'I was taken to meet and – occasionally as a great treat – even to dine with him.'

'Well, fancy,' Johnny said. 'Not that I ever met him.' He opened the book and began to laugh. 'Shall I read this?' he asked. 'Or does it madden you – being read at?'

'Not the bits you read,' I said. 'I'm only amazed at how you instantly seem to find extraordinary innuendo wherever you look.'

'Well, this is harmless; oh, hold hard, as the bishop said,

maybe it isn't – it's about the old bird called the Marchesa Lulie Torrigiani. No, it's not, I tell a lie, it's a story she told, apparently about two policemen on the prowl for indecent behaviour in a public park. They hid behind a bush and heard a female voice implore, "Oh, do let me take a last look before you put it in." Leaping forth to catch a couple in flagrant delight, they find two old women burying a cat. The judge ruled the arrest was exucontian. He'd want to watch his spelling on that.'

'I don't believe it,' I said. 'Let me see.'

I saw. 'How out of a large book full of decent literary material do you alight on that? And what does exo ...'

Careful, dearie,' he interrupted, 'mind where you put that O or you'll have slipped in, as the actress said. It means "out of nothing", I believe. And it happens quite by chance; the double meanings, I mean. Or perhaps because you're looking for it like the *I Ching* ... not to mention the cling film. Open it anywhere and you come on it. In a manner of speaking.'

'If any of you want to go out for a walk you should go now,' Olive said, appearing in the doorway, her hat squashed down hard on her head. ''Tis stopped raining. Only just, mind, and I shouldn't wonder it will start up again ...'

'Put on your bikini, Olive, and let's go,' Johnny said, lumbering to his feet and kissing her.

'Olive,' piped up Rose, 'What's V-A-G-?'

I seized her book and hid it before they could finish the spelling. The children squealed with rage.

'V-A-G-U-E, darlings,' Johnny said. 'Best thing to be around here.'

'Whatever's wrong with these children?' Olive said. 'Good as gold like the white hen's chickens when I came in. Reading.'

'Mum's took our book,' Rose wailed. 'And it was all about pees –'

'And Qs,' said Johnny. 'Where shall we go for a walk?'

'You could go up to Nibley Knoll,' Olive said, 'afore it rains again.'

'Then our nibbles *will* be knolled,' Johnny said, prancing into the hallway.

Olive and the children dribbled off into the hall to climb into their sou'westers.

Johnny said, puffing out his cheeks, 'She's worth a guinea a box.'

'She's worth what?' I said.

'Told you you were young,' he said. 'It was everywhere. They come as a boon and blessing to men, the something, a hen and a Waverley Pen, they're worth a guinea a box. Those were the good old days, weren't they, Olive?'

'Not for me they weren't, sir,' she said. 'And it were Beechams Pills as were worth a guinea a box.'

'Nor for me, neither,' Johnny said and kissed her.

Now I look back, I think I was young, and I know I was lucky. I'm not young any more and there's less luck and laughter now that Olive's dead and, now, so is Johnny.

WRISTS, MISTS AND POETS

....

'I suppose there *is* an Irish style,' she said, looking around as though it might be misplaced somewhere within the red heart of her exotic, but always impeccable, office. 'Long necks,' she said, 'swans, wrists, Yeats. And, of course, the poetry. The po-et-ree. The Irish open their mouths and poetry comes out.' She looked at me expectantly, but I clamped my lips shut and tried to lift my head further up from between my shoulders, but fear had me in its hunch and the long Irish neck remained hidden.

Wrists? I thought frantically. Wrists? Perhaps she means 'mists'. I couldn't open my mouth, as it was filled with rye bread and tuna, a deadly combination when you're sitting only a couple of feet away across a bridge table from one of the most extraordinary human beings you are ever likely to meet. Her every line looked as though it had been drawn by a Higher Draughtsman, Blake, or Fuseli perhaps, certainly someone not quite right in the mind, but absolutely at home in the further reaches of unhinged imagination. This woman, the editor of *Vogue, my* editor at *Vogue,* Diana Vreeland, who lived a life predicated on 'line, style, cut,' was not the easiest person with whom to share a working lunch. I use the term 'share' loosely. She ate practically nothing (always more or less the same sandwich) and downed a slug of scotch.

She may have believed her office wasn't exotic – ('I hate exoticism because it's so silly; my office – just a big, black lacquer desk, a leopard-skin carpet, leopard-skin upholstery, and scarlet walls') – but then she believed whatever she wanted to believe. If this wasn't exotic then what would exotic be? I wanted to clutch my neckless head. But exotic or not, her office and lunch table were an education in formality and exactitude. Here was a woman who had a map of her desk so that everything on it would always be in exactly the same place. Not me though. I seemed to spread like Asia over the map, and every week I tried to think of something to eat that would somehow be tidy. I didn't care about nourishment or taste. I just wanted not to have to dribble or chew or rescue things from about my face. Food took on its own crazed space-life in her room; at her card table, yogurt dribbled, tuna splatted, hamburger fed my frocks, crackers crumbled down the cleavage, a BLT made me look as though I had just been prodded out of a pen with a well-warned vet in attendance. But she and I had this regular eat-feast forum on the eighteenth floor of the Graybar Building on Lexington Avenue, in order for Mrs Vreeland to tap into my arcane knowledge of what the trendy young were doing. I had absolutely no idea; but terror, though it made me draw in my neck, loosened my tongue, and a fair few of the items in that famous *Vogue* column, 'People Are Talking About', sprang straight from my crazed, verbal inventions as I sought to unclamp my teeth from a piece of pastrami without her noticing.

'What does "beady" mean?' An old fashion baron was in the office with her; not old-fashioned, you understand. Old in the ways of fashion and infinitely old in age, like something that wandered out of Shangri-La. 'Now this word that's all the rage in London, "beady," Nicky here has no idea about its meaning, have you, Nicky? Nicky's heart is in his icons. But Polly will know.' She bared her wonderful teeth at both of us.

Nicky couldn't have been less interested in a twenty-four year old Irish female. He was hoping Bailey would come rocketing into the office. My ignorance was so wholesale that I knew that in a million years she could have no conception of how little she knew about a lost world that I knew; the world where I had been born and where I grew up, a world which she would have been amazed to know still existed. She would, of course, have sent Irving Penn to photograph it as a witness to a culture on the brink of extinction. Then she wouldn't have used the pictures, since we weren't the mud-people of Lough Neagh, but merely the ragged ends of a dispensation that had lasted for centuries, the world of the horse and cart and silence and lapping water and goodness and madness. It was about to become extinct, but then so was her world if she'd but known it. But in that office our two worlds met as so many did in that extraordinary symbiotic world of *Vogue* in the 1960s.

Her world was all invention, eclecticism, freakishness, style, and narrow to the bone; the world I had come from knew nothing of invention – everything was old, organic, decaying, and the fatter the better; there were a lot of freaks – inbreeding tends towards that, but we didn't, as they say, remark on them. I was, though, inventive. I had to be to survive and so I invented myself and my identity and invented like mad in that office, which has now taken on a legendary status like Chanel's drawingroom in the Rue Cambon or Schiaparelli's Brown Study. And I bridged the gaps with invention and she met me halfway, both of us teetering above the truth. Below were the bodies of the boring.

Whenever I came to lunch I brought with me a copy of her latest memo:

To: Miss Devlin

Re: January I Predictions – Urgent

Each year we have a potpourri of things that are coming up... Last year we had the marvellous sun bathing tub. The year before, a marvellous picture of a surfing movie and one of Ira Furstenburg ... sketches of Courreges as he was then, behind a curtain and now showing, etc. etc. What we need is a kick – a new thing – a thing we predict for 1968. It could be a sport – a game – a point of view – a new word – anything, but we need it and we need it fast ... Do ask the girls around you for something that we could write either in the Predictions – or we could photograph ... They could be small pictures – this is not a thing of great importance – but it is to delight the reader ... It may be a new discovery in the Orient ... Anything ...

'"Beady." It's the new word the young are using,' she said. 'Now the last time that divine Jean was here she said that Bailey was "looking beady". What exactly did she mean?'

I didn't know; or, rather, knowing Jean, I knew that it could mean anything. Bailey's eyes were small and dark and bright and were born beady; and when Jean thought that anyone was looking at her oddly in the street, she'd whisper uneasily, 'Why are people being so beady?'

'They're being beady because they can't believe they're seeing you,' I said. Jean Shrimpton was the most modest woman you could meet and the most famous model of her time and never really took the impact of her looks on board.

At that time Vreeland was in love with both of them, Bailey

and Shrimpton, as she was in love with so much that was beautiful and new. 'I loathe nostalgia,' she said. 'I don't believe in anything before penicillin.' (Yet when she went back, after her husband's death, and looked at the house near Regent's Park in London where they had lived as newly marrieds, she desperately wanted to have the knocker on the door. She'd bought it on their honeymoon. But perhaps such impulses are not nostalgia, but rather emotion and sensibility. Certainly even when she became an old, almost blind, woman, running the Costume Institute at the Metropolitan Museum of Art in New York and making the most tremendous go of it, she was surrounded by the young and the talented who admired her and recognised how unique she was; how her life and art ran in delightful, ornamented channels.)

She had no simplicity and little amplitude. But you don't need these qualities to be editor of *Vogue*. And she wasn't interested in the dark swirls of the unconscious. She was surface, surface, surface. But what a surface.

'What is swan-upping?' she said. 'I want you to go and talk to the swan-uppers of England. All the property of the Queen, of course, and if you kill a swan you can be beheaded. Absolute, as it should be.'

'What is swan-upping?' I said. I was faltering fast.

'Well, I believe it's turning the swan, that sublime creature, over – upsadaisy – and marking it, tenderly, I hope; the divine right of kings or queens and its wonderful flurry of white, white feathers and long necks and costumes like Beefeaters. On the Avon, I believe. I want wonderful text, wonderful photographs.'

Swan-upping? Where do you start?

She had first come into my life, like a genie, via a cable to British *Vogue*, where I had just started work. It was my first job and I was absolutely penniless. I had come straight from Ardboe, a tiny almost medieval place on the shores of Lough Neagh in Northern

Ireland (loosely and erroneously called Ulster), where a copy of *Vogue* was a fairly *recherché* object. All the same I contrived to get it, a month late, on special order from Sheehy's in Cookstown, and read it as I might read an archive from the future. In one January issue there was a talent contest; the prize, a job at *Vogue*. Jacqueline Kennedy had once won it, the legend said, as had Penelope Gilliat. One had married the President of the US, the other, my hero, John Osborne. The closing date for entries was three days away by then so I wrote the answers fairly sharpish (one question was to write an autobiography, a fairly hubristic endeavor for a twenty year old), and I won; on energy and impetus I should think, the noble savage on a roll. I started work at *Vogue*, in Hanover Square, London, in 1963, and my salary was ten pounds a week regardless of how much I wrote or published. *Vogue* owned all rights. I didn't realise this.

Within six months of my arrival at *Vogue*, and due to a series of sackings rather than to any rocket-like brilliance on my part, I became features editor; also caption writer, commissioning editor and features writer. In those days the features department consisted of me, a secretary shared with the travel department (one person), and an assistant. We worked till we dropped. And then one fine day, soon after I had arrived, a cable came into the office from American *Vogue*. It said simply: 'Osborne/Devlin text superb. $500 for first American rights. D.V.'

The Osborne text was my first interview. John Osborne's play *Look Back in Anger*, first staged a few years before, had changed the course of English theatre history, blah, blah, and to many young people he was a hero and champion. But he'd made himself public enemy number one to many more conservative people when he'd written an angry, polemical letter to the *Tribune*, an English newspaper, now defunct:

> This is a letter of hate. It is for you, my countrymen. I
> mean those men of my country who have defiled it.
> The men with manic fingers leading the sightless,
> feeble, betrayed body of my country to its death.
> Damn you, England, you're nothing now and quite
> soon you'll disappear.

I loved his letter. just what I'd have liked to have said myself,
though from other motives. But after its publication a storm
erupted, he was threatened with death, and had gone to ground.
So when I wrote asking for an interview I didn't have much hope
he'd give one. In any case it never occurred to me that I could
actually talk to a hero. Might as well expect the blue and white
statue in the chapel at home to suddenly flounce down onto the
altar. So it was a fair old turn-up when I got a sweet note
suggesting we meet for lunch. He talked all afternoon. Osborne
was a wonderful talker, witty and biting and no-holds-barred. I
wrote the article. It was published in British *Vogue*, and then the
magic cable, trailing stardust, arrived. My stock rose within the
office, since American *Vogue* was jealous of its commissioning
originality and rarely lifted pieces from other magazines in the
Condé Nast family. I was puffed up with pride, but the pride was as
nothing compared to the prospect of five hundred dollars for those
mysterious first American rights.

Five hundred dollars then was the equivalent of six months'
salary, but it was much more than that to me. It was a recognition
that I could write, that my writing was worth something, that
people would pay to read it. The managing director of English
Vogue cabled back and told them that they already owned all
rights so I didn't need payment. But that first enabling cable was
from Diana Vreeland and I loved her for it. And now here was the
reality in front of me. Using the word 'reality' loosely, you

understand, because she was as fantastical as a unicorn, as flash as a kingfisher on that cold, gray day in 1964 when London was in mourning for Winston Churchill

Our offices at *Vogue* were open plan, with partitions and bookcases about shoulder height. I was sitting sucking my teeth, when this extraordinary apparition came bobbing, or rather gliding, along above the level of the filing cabinets – the wonderful carved head of a totem pole perhaps, or an Aztec bird woman, or a Kabuki runaway. It's a famous image now, that carrowary head, that stretch of the face. But when it first came, disembodied, into my life, along the line of a gray London corridor, it was like a religious visitation, my own personal Fatima. And its voice was booming, ricocheting around, a boomerang going back to its sender, only to be spun away again, bearing another sibylline pronouncement. Then she appeared through the gap in the cabinets and threw up her hands. There's a word not much used nowadays, 'limned,' which means 'to illuminate, to edge in colour'. She was always limned, set in shock against her background. You could hardly see her for the dazzle – the huge mouth; the high, bright-red cheeks; the burnishing black-on-black lacquered hair; the edge and cut and glitter of her chic, the slanting, knowing eyes like a fox-terrier's, missing many a thing to do with the soul, but nothing, nothing to do with the body. To me she was so ugly, I couldn't believe it. Five minutes later the ugliness had vanished under the fascination. The way she stood was unique. Cecil Beaton famously described it: 'the Vreeland medieval slouch, pelvis thrust forward to an astonishing degree and the torso above it sloping backwards at a forty-five degree angle'. She was offering me a job on *Vogue* in New York and while doing so talked non-stop, examining me with her twinkling eyes. And twinkle they did; and glitter, like tiny light bulbs flashing, taking an infinite series of shots, and editing down into what *she* wanted to see. In the process she missed a lot, but what she missed, she thought she didn't want. Her vision ignored the ordinary.

But, of course, one of the things that made her extraordinary was that she never tried to be fanatical, or larger than life. It was all natural to her, if the word 'natural' could ever have been used within her aura. She said, 'I figure that if I like something, the rest of the world will like it too. I think I have an absolutely solid ordinary point of view.' True eccentrics do think what they do and how they think are perfectly normal. Perfect, yes. Normal, no. Her account of the last evening she spent in Paris in September 1939, when one of the world's greatest calamities was beginning, and when she knew she was leaving it, perhaps for the last time (and she loved Paris as others love lovers) reveals a mind-set that is almost frightening in its lack of grasp on horrid reality. She went walking up and down the Champs Élysées with a friend. 'We must have walked ten miles that night … and hundreds of people were strolling but they hardly spoke, only this unearthly silence … I can remember exactly what I was wearing: a little black tallieur from Chanel, a little piece of black lace wrapped around my head, and absolutely exquisite black kid slippers.'

Verbal textures, strange priorities, nothing rough. Anyone else might have given a gloss to the moment, spoken of their emotions, about their sense of despair, of apprehension or being part of a historic moment. But what she wore informed her memory of occasion. There is no right or wrong in chic. And her refusal or inability to turn her back on anything that seemed chic or stylish, no matter how mendacious, was what made her, in my eyes, an amoral woman. She would ask me to go and interview people who smelled of badness, a rank smell of horrid sex, money and mendacity, chicanery and foolishness, but they were stylish so she admired them. And I would go. I would go. I would register my displeasure. 'Oh, you just want to ride the tiger's back,' she said. I had no idea what she meant, or pretended I didn't. But I had bought into the deal; virtue was not necessarily something to be admired and style was. 'Be stylish, young maid, and let who will be good ...' Nothing was allowed to interfere with her idea of style: she hated liars but she herself invented the truth.

Listening to her talking about clothes was to hear voluptuous pleasure and delight in the art of clothes, of textures and sheens and fabrics. She talked about colour like no-one else: 'When I say orange, I don't mean yellow-orange, I mean red-orange, the orange of Bakst and Diaghilev, the orange that changed the century'; or 'The best red to copy is the color of any child's cap in any Renaissance portrait.' She returned from South America and crooned: '... a world of youth with long oval faces, long waving arms like the palm trees along their long waving coastline.'

She set ground rules that were hard to preempt. 'The first thing to do is to arrange to be born in Paris. After that everything follows naturally.' I'd fallen at the first fence. Ardboe was the antithesis of Paris. Fashion there depended on how the priest wore his biretta. And I knew that the space between what she thought was natural and I thought was natural was a chasm into which we would both fall if we just once peeked. So I clamped my teeth over my sandwich and kept mum about my background. But, in any case, she wasn't interested. She filleted people for what they could give her not for what they were. She invented me for herself. 'She sprang from nowhere, the wilds of Ireland,' she told Nicky, who stared out of her window down Lexington, where there wasn't a pretty boy in sight. 'I discovered her writing this proooose, you know, about Osborne and the poets, one of the great playwrights of England.' The wilds of Ireland, tiny farms, hens in the rampar, ceaseless rain, the rushes along the lough shore, the misery of school in Magherafelt, the fashion as revealed in the Drapery in Cookstown – the realities of a world where there was no such word as elegance or luxury. I thought about her practical early DIY [Do It Yourself] tips in *Harper's Bazaar* and how useful they would be in my own dear family life in County Tyrone. 'Why don't you sweep into your drawingroom on your first big night with an enormous red fox muff of many skins … knit yourself a little skull-cap … turn your old ermine coat into a bathrobe … tie black tulle bows on your wrist …' Thinking about it I burst out laughing and the old baron turned round just in time to see me choke into the Dixie cup.

Over the two years I worked for her, I lost my terror of her. What helped was that I knew that this woman, whose style was in the cut of her vision, was also ridiculous and often unintentionally funny. But she could miss the point by a mile and still arrive on target.

She was determined that no-one would think she wasn't serious or hard-working. 'Never be deceived into thinking that the life of fashion was easy. It was exhausting. After a day of fitting you crept to your dark room.' (A dark room that contained a highly-trained maid and often a manicurist and masseur to restore herself to herself.) I thought of the dark rooms at home lit by oil lamps and grinned with pleasure that it was all behind me, and I thought perhaps next time I had lunch I could order something I could suck through a straw, or bring a bullet and bite on it when she started to praise some pretty, druggy layabout who wasn't worth a hill of beans, but had a lot of *chutzpah* and a good line in cross-dressing.

She was funny, sharp, with a tongue quick as a lizard's. She rolled-up words to create images. Once she set her fashion editors searching for a new miracle fabric called 'Chelanayzee' or thereabouts. Defeated in their search, the fashion editors did a bit of lateral thinking and came up with Celanese.

She also tried to make the photographers who worked for her create the images she wanted. 'Don't you adore the look of white silk slippers with the dark hem of a velvet dress? The Eskimos, I'm told, have seventeen different words for shades of white. This is even more than there are in *my* imagination.' I once told her that there was no word for 'no' in the Irish language but a thousand ways of saying 'yes'. She was enchanted.

Diana Vreeland became editor of American *Vogue* in 1962 after twenty-eight years of working for *Harper's Bazaar*. ('They gave me a raise of a thousand dollars. Can you imagine? Would you give your cook that after that many years?') My cook? Hello? Are you in there somewhere, Mrs Vreeland? I once asked her how much she thought she'd changed *Vogue*. She said, 'By the time I hit the place everyone looked great. The boys inspired the girls, the boys were nuts about the girls. The girls were nuts about the boys. I don't say it was great photography, but it was the photography of the hour.'

All the same she did change *Vogue*, sending it into a spin of extravagance, exaggeration and fantasy. She loved the whole youth thing to a fault, and the aloof, *soignée* beauties of tradition in *Vogue* disappeared, to be replaced by something called the 'youth-quake', a word she coined to describe new movements and trends. She was unembarrassed in her invention of labels and names like this, making anyone with any sense cringe. Thus the 'Beautiful People' became a cliché for a certain style of mondane and would-be mondane life in the 1960s. 'I hate to see the term mis-used,' she complained. 'We mean people who are beautiful to look at. It's been taken up to mean people who are rich. We mean charmers but there is no harm in being rich.' Each issue of *Vogue* was like her newborn baby, and she behaved towards the finished issue rather like a father staring at his young; wondering how that conception, by now a remote pleasure, should have resulted in this?

Her bosses at *Vogue* seem to have been equally startled and less pleased. It made for exciting times. Alexander Liberman, for years the *Vogue* supremo, wasn't a great fan. The crux of the matter was whether *Vogue* was a magazine of record and fashion, showing what women might wear in their ideal and perfectly groomed lives, or a magazine of Diana Vreeland's conception, a place for the wildest of dreams. 'Vreeland was one of the editors who really struggled with photographers, to make them bring out what she thought was fascinating in fashion,' he once said. 'And the photographers would consider that they were taking a picture. It made for great conflict. With Diana Vreeland it was a struggle; she would sometimes make photographers re-take three or four times, which could be agony for many. The result was often wonderful, but at the same time it was quite destructive photographically. Because the final image was unspontaneous, unreal – it was the twentieth image and even then it was retouched, so it was very artificial. She was trying to get a certain essence of fashion into each picture.'

Certain photographers adored her but others were driven into hysterics. 'She'd look at the clothes and then drift into a sort of trance,' one said. '"I see white," she'd moan, swaying about like Madame Arcati. Or she'd wind a length of hair around a girl's neck, around, around, nearly strangling her, and she'd be saying, "It's Undine, water, naiads,"– and the girl's eyes were popping.'

Those who did not know her often thought that she was affected, but her affectations were intrinsic and, paradoxically, normal to her. That her observations and behaviour had a startling effect on others surprised her; or so she pretended, since surprise wasn't an emotion high on her agenda. Honesty was.

'Chanel once said I was the most pretentious woman she'd ever met. But that was Coco; not a kind woman.'

It would be easy to make her sound like a snob, but the famous names in her lexicon were all her friends. 'I believe totally in romance, love, pleasure and beauty,' she said. 'Anyone who's afraid and does not search and give as much as possible to the world of pleasure is a totally ingrown person.' Well, for such a thing to be said to a convent-educated Irish girl, who had been taught that pleasure made your private parts drop off, fairly made the world rock on its hinges.

After a while she stopped sending me to interview Eurotrash and sent me into the homelands as it were; to Barbados to talk to Oliver Messel; to Maryland to talk to Eunice Shriver; to Paris with Avedon and Barbara Streisand to do the Collections; to Iran to talk to Empress Farah Diba; to San Francisco to talk to Janis Joplin; to 14th Street to listen to Aretha Franklin; to Houston Street to listen to a group of hairy people rehearsing a strange, anarchic, joyous musical, tentatively called *Hair*. At lunchtimes we would all troop up to a fashionable East Side doctor to have a massive injection in our bums to give us energy. B12, I think it was called. I thought it was great; a far cry from Dr Brown's brown and buff surgery in Coagh. Every time I came back there would be the dreaded lunch, and praise. Always praise.

'The sixties were an extraordinary period,' she said. 'It was the youth-quake, it was the pill, and that released a whole different association between the boys and girls and created an entirely different society. Everybody, everything was new, and you were knocked in the eye-balls. For the first time youth went out to life instead of waiting for life to come to them, which is the big difference between the sixties and any other decade I have ever lived in. And don't forget we were at war all the time – and the horrible truth is that people thrive in war, industry, money, spirits and fortunes. It's invigorating, but it's terrible, it mustn't happen again.'

She had a fantastic, beckoning eye for the immediate future; the future of two or three issues away. One of her secrets was that nothing was unattainable – you just had to streettch to get it. Just saying a word like 'stretch' would lead directly to a feature on Martha Graham. She created the needs of her readers and then fulfilled those needs. Looking back at that marvellous time at *Vogue*, one sees that she created a monument, albeit a folly, to a certain time in New York. With four to five hundred pages in each issue, they were high-rolling, ridiculous magazines with their own irresistible snobbery, their own passwords, their own exclusively beautiful people. Within the pages of *Vogue*, *no* matter what reality was doing outside, the denizens danced in the ethnic temples that were their homes, in flowing chiffon pyjamas and chain mail and hair-pieces a foot high and a foot wide and jewellery like treasure trove from under the sea. And the women looked good too. The Vietnam war was ripping the US apart but Diana Vreeland lived in a place where the young were about to conquer everything; where the best season ever for exciting colours and new styles of living was just around the corner. 'It was a very theatrical moment, everyone was theatrical. We had every pretty girl in the world, don't you think?'

For me, Diana Vreeland was the Imprimatur, the Governor, the Ultimate Boss, and the Arbiter of Style. So it was with some bemusement that I discovered that this was not necessarily everyone else's view. At about this time, I married an Englishman, a man whose godparents and their friends had great dynastic American names, like Pell, Bigelow, Whitney and Drexel. Once, while staying in Hobe Sound, or lunching at the Knickerbocker Club or wherever the publicity-shy (Yes!) wives of these quiet, 'old money' Americans gathered in their beleaguered herds, I launched into a eulogy of Diana Vreeland, and saw something I'd never seen before, never even considered a possibility. These women not only did not like her, they did not rate her, and hated what had happened to *Vogue*. Later I mentioned these women to Diana Vreeland. 'Dinosaurs, darling,' she said, 'Dinosaurs. Their day is over – if they ever had a day – which I am inclined to doubt.'

Soon afterwards I left New York and went back to London.

Not just a day, but a whole era was over. Diana Vreeland was sacked. *Vogue* became more prosaic. Her extravagant style was seen as inappropriate for the 1970s. Devastated she might have been, but indomitable as ever, she never faltered. At the Metropolitan Museum of Art, she embarked on a spectacularly successful career as special consultant to the Costume Institute. Shows of period costumes from Russia, from Hollywood, from Paris – which she conceived and organised – were the social events of the season. 'Four hundred thousand people in the basement of the Metropolitan Museum. You've got to say it's quite something.' She was quite something, like no-one else, ever.

And I never did solve the problem of what to eat when I was with her. Years and years later, we had supper in the Plaza Athenée in Paris. I ordered fettucine. I had come a long way. I knew I could eat pasta and talk to Diana Vreeland at the same time. Half an hour later, almost paralysed, I was still rolling the pasta around the fork and the plate. 'I've always said it,' she said, 'but I'll say it again. The Spanish are dervishes compared to you Celts. No sense of time. Wrists, mists, poets. I'm moving on to the next course.' She laughed, that big, loud, lovely laugh that rang down the halls of fashion and style of the twentieth century, and lifted it in a way it has never been lifted before or since.